Jihad

Jihad

A Short History

Terry Bushell

First published in Great Britain in 2022 by
Pen & Sword History
An imprint of
Pen & Sword Books Ltd
Yorkshire – Philadelphia

Copyright © Terry Bushell 2022

ISBN 978 1 39907 357 8

The right of Terry Bushell to be identified as Author of this work has been asserted by him in accordance with the Copyright, Designs and Patents Act 1988.

A CIP catalogue record for this book is available from the British Library.

All rights reserved. No part of this book may be reproduced or transmitted in any form or by any means, electronic or mechanical including photocopying, recording or by any information storage and retrieval system, without permission from the Publisher in writing.

Typeset by Mac Style
Printed in the UK by CPI Group (UK) Ltd, Croydon, CR0 4YY.

Pen & Sword Books Limited incorporates the imprints of Atlas, Archaeology, Aviation, Discovery, Family History, Fiction, History, Maritime, Military, Military Classics, Politics, Select, Transport, True Crime, Air World, Frontline Publishing, Leo Cooper, Remember When, Seaforth Publishing, The Praetorian Press, Wharncliffe Local History, Wharncliffe Transport, Wharncliffe True Crime and White Owl.

For a complete list of Pen & Sword titles please contact

PEN & SWORD BOOKS LIMITED
47 Church Street, Barnsley, South Yorkshire, S70 2AS, England
E-mail: enquiries@pen-and-sword.co.uk
Website: www.pen-and-sword.co.uk

Or

PEN AND SWORD BOOKS
1950 Lawrence Rd, Havertown, PA 19083, USA
E-mail: Uspen-and-sword@casematepublishers.com
Website: www.penandswordbooks.com

Contents

Chapter 1	Massacre of the Jews; the rampages of Khalid	1
Chapter 2	Ukba rides into the Atlantic; Musa conquers Spain; the reigns of al-Mansur, Harun Rashid, al-Mutasim; *mamlukes*; *takiya*; the devastation of India; Arslan, the Battle of Didgori	29
Chapter 3	Hulagu and Baybars; Othman founds the Ottoman empire; dhimmitude; Janibeg, the pioneer of biological warfare, infects Europe with the Black Death; Murad I and Bayezid I; the Siege of Rhodes; creation of the Janissary corps; the Battle of Kosovo; Tamerlane; Mehmed II and the fall of Constantinople	62
Chapter 4	Suleiman I and the Battle of Mohács	120
Chapter 5	Barbarossa; the 1565 Siege of Malta; the conquest of Cyprus; the Battle of Lepanto; the 1683 Siege of Vienna	133

Quotes from the Koran	170
Quotes on Islam	172
Bibliography	174
Index	177

Chapter 1

Massacre of the Jews; the rampages of Khalid

Yathrib, a sprawling fertile agricultural oasis in western Arabia famed throughout the peninsula for its dark succulent ajwa dates, was in the early seventh century home to several wealthy tribes, three of them Jewish. By 627, however, only one Jewish tribe, the Korayza, remained. The other two had been driven out by the practitioners of a new intolerant religious cult, the Hanifiya, who had grown in numbers and power. The Hanifs believed they were following the 'pure religion' of the first monotheist, Abraham.

The Korayza then made a catastrophic mistake. Despite having a non-aggression pact with the Hanifiya they sided with the Hanifiya's enemies, whose coalition army besieged Yathrib in an attempt to destroy the Hanifiya. Appalling weather forced the army to retreat.

The Korayza gathered in their fortress and awaited Hanifiya revenge. When they saw from the battlements an advance guard of the Hanifiya forces plant the Hanifiya war banner at a nearby well they knew a siege was being prepared. Description of what happened next comes from a canonical source, the chronicle of eighth-century historian al-Waqidi, *Book of History and Campaigns*.

The Jews shouted insults and threats. The attackers shouted back, 'We will not leave your fortress until you die of starvation.' The main force arrived by the hundreds over the next few hours and soon totalled 3,000 fighters, heavily armed with the accoutrements of war. Fifty archers went forward and shot volleys of arrows. The Jews shot back. The shooting continued until dark. The attackers spent the night raiding the Jews' ajwa date plantations and eating the succulent fruit. Strengthened and exhilarated by the feast of their foes' famous valuable farm produce, they resumed the siege in the morning.

2 Jihad

The Jews were outnumbered and lacked adequate provisions. Their situation was hopeless. After twenty days they sent one of their noblemen with an offer to surrender if they were allowed to simply leave the oasis as had the other two Jewish tribes. The offer was refused. When the nobleman returned to the fortress with the bad news, he and the other leaders considered their options. One was to convert to the new religion. This would automatically ensure their safety. Many in Yathrib had become nominal members of the cult in order to escape persecution. But that idea was rejected. They would prefer to die faithful to the Torah and the religion of Moses and their ancestors. Another idea revealed the depth of their desperation: to do as the Jewish rebel holdouts at the mountaintop fortress of Masada had done after the destruction of Jerusalem, when the rebels chose mass suicide to deprive the besieging Romans of the satisfaction of butchering them individually. But the Korayza considered this idea repugnant, as it meant that they themselves would have to kill their women and children.

The leaders finally decided that the only recourse was to throw themselves at the mercy of the Hanifs. Hoping for the best, but expecting the worst, the Jews surrendered the next day. The Hanifs separated the men from the women and children, which did not augur well. Sometimes with a male adolescent they had to make a snap decision as to which group he belonged, men or boys, and some tall 14-year-olds were put in among the men while small 17-year-olds were placed in the other group. Boys were considered adult if they had reached puberty. Occasionally there would be a check for pubic hair. Fluffy down was a conundrum, requiring consultation with Hanif colleagues.

Eventually the Hanifs had 900 adult male captives. As these Korayza men filed out of the fortress their hands were tied and they were forced to stand in the scorching sun. They were then roped together and marched to a fortress near the centre of Yathrib. The women and children, about a thousand in all, were taken to a compound. The contents of the Jews' fortress and the other properties of their territory were inventoried for future distribution as booty. In the fortress were found 1,500 swords, 300 suits of armour, 1,000 lances and 1,500 shields and, in the lodgings, fine furniture and silver utensils. The conquerors also uncovered amphorae containing wine. The contents were spilled out (Hanifs had been told to stop going to prayers drunk) and the huge jars kept as booty. Of even greater value was the property of the Jews' territory, the accumulated wealth of generations: blockhouses and villages, barley fields and the precious ajwa date plantations.

The Hanifs condemned the 900 men to death by decapitation. They dug a trench in a main market-place that would be long enough and wide enough to accommodate the bodies. The work began after breakfast. It took until the early afternoon for the trench to be completed. The captives were then fetched for execution. They had spent the night praying, reciting the Torah and encouraging each other to find strength in their faith. When the time for their deaths arrived they were hustled out of their fortress prison, six at a time. Hands bound behind them, they were marched to the market-place, led to the edge of the trench, forced to their knees and decapitated by a sword. Some who had been wearing expensive garments when captured ripped them in many places so they would have no value as booty. Others, with clothes worth preserving, were forced to take them off, so that some of them died naked.

The executioners would ask their victims to make it easy on themselves by bending their necks forward. This was more for their own benefit than the victim, as they did not want to have to make multiple swings to get a head off. Often, they had a Jew who had fallen on his side shrieking and writhing in agony. They would then have to either get him back on to his knees to get the job done or hack his head off while he lay on his side. And too many people needed to be slain to waste time on niceties.

Rarely is execution by beheading achieved with a single stroke. One exception was that of Anne Boleyn in the Tower of London, who, like the Yathrib Jews, was kneeling upright – but the man who had condemned her, her husband Henry the Eighth, had hired an expert swordsman from France to ensure a clean, tidy, swift death. More typical was the execution in the Tower of another Henry VIII victim, Catholic martyr Margaret Pole, Countess of Salisbury, five years later. Savoyard ambassador Eustace Chapuys described it: 'A wretched and blundering youth literally hacked her head and shoulders to pieces in the most pitiful manner.' And sixty years later, also in the Tower, Robert Devereux, Earl of Essex, condemned to execution for treason, too was hacked to death. Lytton Strachey describes it in his biography *Elizabeth and Essex*: the executioner 'whirled up the axe, and crashed it downwards; the body made no movement; but twice more the violent action was repeated before the head was severed and the blood poured forth.' Another victim during Elizabeth's reign, her cousin, Mary, Queen of Scots, also needed three blows. The first missed her neck and struck the back of her head. The second severed the neck except for a small bit of sinew, which the executioner cut through. (When he held up her head the auburn tresses in his hand turned out to be a wig, which he was left holding while the head fell to the ground, revealing that Mary had grey hair even though she was only 44.)

And at least some of the victims at Yathrib must have tried to escape. These would have suffered horrific wounds on their upper torso until they fell to the ground when a Hanif would frantically chop at the neck, clumsily, obliquely, angered when at last the head came off because his blade would then slam into the stony ground, potentially dulling or chipping it, and he had many more victims to slay. Korayza men wore their hair long, and hair also quickly blunted swords. The ground by the mass grave pit must have been drenched with blood and gore on which the doomed captives, their guards, the executioners and the assistants grotesquely slipped and slithered.

The assistants swung the torsos in the trench in such a way that it was filled evenly. Down in the trench, torsos and limbs were sprawled, and sandwiched in between were the heads, all with severed necks exposed. Though the victims were at the height of terror at the moment of death, the severing of their necks relaxed the muscles and gave their faces the appearance of repose, as if they had fallen asleep.

None of the Jews begged for mercy or fainted but some lost control of their bowels, while others were in a semi-conscious state of shock, and many wept with grief as they knelt at the edge of the trench with their arms painfully tied behind them and gazed down at the bodies and severed heads of their fathers, sons, brothers, cousins and uncles. A young woman was also executed for having thrown a millstone down from the fortress during the siege, crushing the head of a Hanif who was carried back to the camp where he died three days later. All the other women were forced to watch the executions, along with their children.

This beheading of 900 captives was a massive undertaking, lasting well into the night, the later ones by the light of flickering amber torches. The trench was filled in at dawn. As it had been dug and filled hurriedly, it was too shallow and not covered adequately, so that methane and other gases of putrefaction seeped through the earth and spread like ground mist. The square ceased to serve as a market-place.

Gradually, as the corpses decomposed, the soil subsided. The odour of death persisted for a long time. It was a cursed place reeking of death, the hollowed mass grave and the blood staining the ground perpetual hateful reminders of a cruel, barbaric act. Bloodstains notoriously linger, being hard to wash off clothes, for example, and the square, once a bustling market, was for many years marked with blood. In Yathrib it was the custom for distinctive graves to be dug, different to those in other parts of the region, which were levelled. Yathrib graves had a niche for valued favourite objects of the deceased, and were rounded off tastefully with a mound, for which specialist gravediggers were employed. One is named in records – Abu Talha Zayd bin Sahl. The crude elongated hole in the ground that was the mass grave was a further affront to local sensibilities. People feared ghosts of lost souls. Not only did the square cease to serve as a market-place – the inhabitants of Yathrib avoided it altogether, preferring the longer walk around it rather than going through it.

After the mass grave was filled in the booty had to be distributed. Much of the plunder of property, livestock, weapons and ajwa date plantations was put up for auction but the disposition of a thousand women and children involved complex transactions. They were divided into five portions. A merchant named Abd ar-Rahman, one of the earliest converts to the new religion who had the reputation of being the shrewdest trader and financier, had the funds to buy an entire portion. Two hundred slaves became his property. As an astute businessman, he made a big profit by selling them on.

Traumatised women and children who remained unsold were taken under armed guard to slave markets in the north-east, and the proceeds from their sale were used to buy weapons, camels and horses. Any Hanif warrior would be delighted to obtain a horse because it had recently become Hanifiya policy that a cavalryman received three times the share of booty as a man in the infantry.

The Hanifiya had executed all the Korayza men and sold the women and children into slavery because they were not afraid of any consequences. They had acted entirely in accordance with the customs of the time and region. The only morality was within the tribe, and the Hanifs thought of themselves as a new kind of tribe, one based on religion and not on kinship. This idea was nowhere given theoretical expression but was everywhere implied or assumed. They had no duties or obligations towards members of other tribes, even of common decency, no idea whatsoever of a minimum standard of decent behaviour towards all humans just because they were human. They had no conception of a universal moral law. The only restraints on behaviour towards any outsider were those set by fear of retaliation or fear of supernatural powers. Also, with meat being the main ingredient in the diet and frequent animal sacrifice, slaughter was a big part of Arabs' lives. They lived with butchery. To them, killing was commonplace, a daily occurrence.

Throughout Arabia, Jews continued to oppose the Hanifiya to the best of their ability but in the end their tribes were crushed, the last major confrontation being at Khaybar, an oasis on the western plateau to the north of Yathrib noted for its vegetables, grains, silk garments, metal tools and instruments of war. Six clans allied by blood and religion lived in fortresses and surrounding villages, each with its own fields and plantations. Some of the plantations were enormous. One contained 40,000 palm trees, another 12,000. Because of lack of unity and collaboration between the clans, allowing the Hanifiya to conquer their separate strongholds one by one, they were defeated and became the Hanifs' vassals. Many Jews remained in Arabia, but they ceased to count in Arabian politics and lost much of their wealth.

The Yathrib population, which previously was about 20,000, had been halved by the purge of the Jews, but grew again as converts and chancers arrived from Bedouin tribes. Many Bedouin tribesmen were attracted by the prospect of booty, joining raids and campaigns in hopes of plunder. Historian Sir William Muir wrote in 1861 that the prospect of enrichment fanned a 'zeal for active service'. And the service was indeed active. The need for loot kept raiding parties busy. According to al-Waqidi, one raid targeted a Bedouin clan that roamed the desert highlands sixty miles east of Yathrib and was known to possess numerous livestock. The raiding party of thirty men, led by a commander named Khalid ibn al-Walid, who had already acquired a reputation for bloodthirstiness, took a couple of days on horseback to reach their destination and position themselves for an attack. They stealthily surrounded the Bedouin camp on a clear moonlit night and attacked it in a cavalry charge at dawn, catching their victims wholly by surprise, sleepy and unprepared, and hacking to death all who ran out of their tents to defend themselves. The survivors fled, abandoning 150 camels, 3,000 goats and all their tents and personal belongings. The raiders grabbed everything that could be carried and herded the livestock back to Yathrib.

This was simple unashamed, unadorned banditry. Booty could also be had just by robbing highwaymen of their plunder. Once, hundreds of Hanifs fell without warning on a valley where bandits were grazing stolen livestock. Al-Waqidi wrote that the survivors of the attack 'fled in every direction'.

Other Hanifiya raiding parties sent to destroy pagan sanctuaries or forcibly convert pagan or Christian tribes combined missionary zeal with mercenary avarice. One had as its objective the subjugation of the Christian tribe of Dumat al-Jandal, whose sandstone market town bordered on Syria 500 miles north of Yathrib, an important trade centre on the east-west caravan route that linked the Red Sea to the Persian Gulf. To reach it, the raiding party of 700 men led by the merchant ar-Rahman had to cross the Nafud sand dunes of the Najd desert. As well as the subjugation of a Christian tribe, the expedition also marked an early stage in the growth of intense Hanifiya interest in the route to the north and Syria.

Ar-Rahman had been ordered to wage *jihad*, holy war, against the tribe, to fight everyone obstructing Allah and to kill those who disbelieved in Allah. The Christians, knowing that the Hanifs had massacred the Korayza Jews earlier that year, took the threat of slaughter seriously but proposed that all their men pay protection money in the form of a new poll tax called *jizya* to remain Christian. Ar-Rahman accepted this proposal. Being a merchant, he was accustomed to making deals, and was pleased with this one. He sealed the agreement by marrying the chief's daughter Tumadir, as instructed – a political marriage, common in the lawless land of delicate alliances. He returned to Yathrib with Tumadir and the first payment of the *jizya* tax.

The word *jizya* is believed to have come from a similar Syriac word meaning poll tax, either directly or through Persian, but it might also be an Arabic formation meaning 'due' or 'satisfaction'.

The first sanctuary idol to fall was that of the mother-goddess al-Uzza. To worship her was to worship the energy that animated all life. Her sanctuary at Nakhl, Palm Valley, south of Yathrib, was a modest temple erected on a hillside amid a cluster of ancient acacia trees. Khalid led his thirty men to it. He knew it from childhood. His father used to make pilgrimages there to sacrifice camels and goats at the altar, and Khalid and his siblings had often taken part. When the adult Khalid arrived with his raiders, all but one of the people at the sanctuary fled up the hillside. An Abyssinian woman, either a devotee or a priestess, ran out screaming at him. Despite it being a sanctuary, Khalid attacked her with his sword and, according to reports, 'cut her in two'. He and his men destroyed the temple, chopped down its ancient acacia trees and took everything they could plunder.

On his return from that raid, Khalid led a detachment of light cavalry, 350 men, to a Red Sea tribe, the Jadhima, acting as a missionary though most of the tribe had already converted. The literature states:

> When the tribesmen of Jadhima saw him they grasped their weapons, and Khalid said, 'Put down your weapons, for everyone has accepted Hanifiya.' A man named Jahdam said, 'Woe to you, Jadhima! This is Khalid. If you put down your weapons you will be bound, and after you have been bound you will be beheaded. I will never put down my weapons.' Some of his people laid hold of

him, saying, 'Do you want to shed our blood? Everyone else has accepted Hanifiya and put down their weapons; war is over and everyone is safe.' They persisted to the point of taking away his weapons, and they themselves put down their arms at Khalid's word. As soon as they had put down their weapons Khalid ordered their hands to be tied behind their backs and slew them, killing thirty of them.

Apparently this savage massacre was in revenge for the murder of one of Khalid's uncles by Jadhima tribesmen several years before.

Before the slayings Jahdam said, 'Jadhima, I gave you full warning of the disaster into which you have fallen.' He was among those slain – as was a woman who had supported him in his warning, one of two women to die.

The other died of a broken heart. A cavalryman named Yakub who was with Khalid said,

A young man of the Jadhima who was about my own age spoke to me. His hands were tied to his neck by an old rope and the women were standing in a group a short distance away. He asked me to take hold of the rope and lead him to the women so that he might say to one of them what he had to say and then bring him back and do what we liked with him. I said that that was a small thing to ask and I led him to them. As he stood by them he said to a girl, 'Fare you well, Hubaysha, though my life is at an end.'

Then Yakub took him away and he was beheaded by another young Muslim horseman who, standing behind him, said to the doomed innocent youth with a show of compassion, 'Do not be afraid' before lethally swinging his sword. Two gruesome entities lay on the sandy ground. Yakub said that Hubaysha screamed and went to her beloved 'and bent over him and kept on kissing him until she died at his side' without adding the grisly detail as to whether she kissed the severed head or the separate torso, from which the marrow was welling up from the vertebrae.

One numerous tribe, the Hawazin, whose territory straddled the caravan route leading to the Persian Gulf in the east, were committed to their polytheist beliefs and, when they heard of the Hanifs' genocidal extermination of pagan tribes, feared they would soon be targeted and resolved to launch a pre-emptive strike. The Hanifs, too, decided attack was the best form of defence and the two forces clashed at the entrance to a rugged, uninhabited valley called Hunayn, the Hawazin joined by allies from the walled mountain town of Taif. The coalition was united under the leadership of Malik Awf, a chieftain of a Hawazin clan. Although only 30, he was a renowned warrior and an eloquent speaker. Against the advice of older sheikhs, he took along and kept in the rear of the army all the women and children and all the tribal possessions, including vast herds of camels and goats, to give the warriors motivation to fight to the death if necessary, for not only would they be fighting against the hated enemy, but they would also be fighting to protect their loved ones.

In the event, the coalition soldiers, overwhelmed by a numerically superior force, broke and ran, leaving the women, children and livestock defenceless. The Hanifiya army captured 6,000 women and children, 24,000 camels and 40,000 sheep and goats. They were taken to a valley called Jirana to be held until they could be disposed of. All the men who were captured or surrendered were executed.

The Hanifiya army then besieged Taif, the defenders sending down showers of arrows and red-hot metal, and more than a month went by before the condition of the 6,000 captives was considered. They had been kept out in the open all that time, as in a refugee camp devoid of shelter, and fed by the guards only because if they starved to death they could not be sold as slaves. The captors kept the rations to an absolute minimum, however, as more than sixty animals had to be slaughtered every day, reducing daily the livestock available as loot.

When the human and animal captives were finally parcelled out, Hanifiya warriors and prominent believers such as the merchant ar-Rahman were each allocated a female. Some sent theirs to a relation to hold until it was confirmed she was definitely not pregnant. Al-Waqidi wrote of one virgin, 'She was a pure and admirable slave girl.' After a few months, Taif surrendered through conversion and the Hanifiya leaders made peace with Malik, signing an agreement that included returning the Hawazin females to their homeland. Naturally the Hanifiya warriors and prominent believers objected but were persuaded to comply and the women and girls were sent home – many of them now indeed pregnant.

Fourteenth-century scholar Tafsir ibn Kathir wrote that on surrendering by converting the Taif citizens requested that they be allowed to keep their beloved goddess al-Lat for three years and that the request was refused: her sanctuary, temple and all personal idols of her had to be destroyed immediately. As they would baulk at destroying the temple with their own hands, a small force of ten heavily armed men destroyed it for them, led by a top Hanif from Taif named Mughira, who was a fugitive and desperado in the eyes of the people of the town for murdering thirteen of his tribesmen and stealing their merchandise. Choosing him as the foreman of the demolition squad clearly was designed to deepen the townspeople's degradation. Nobody dared to challenge the squad. The temple's al-Lat idol, carved of white stone with inscriptions, was behind curtains. Mughira and his men smashed it to pieces with pickaxes and sledgehammers, then levelled the temple, keeping all the gold, silver, perfume, fabric and everything else of value they came across. Ibn Kathir wrote that the citizens wept as the goddess of fertility worshipped in the town for centuries was reduced to rubble.

The Hanifiya then completed the conquest of north-west Arabia, before targeting the southern part of the peninsula for further expansion, as usual employing the tactic of shock-and-awe, 'making slaughter in the land', as they put it, to undermine the will to resist. With this tactic, they subjugated the religious and commercial centre of an entire region of Yemen, which was noted throughout the peninsula. After that Khalid usually had only to show up at the head of a cavalry force and the targeted population would surrender, as happened when he stopped at the gate of the Christian town of Najran and called out, 'Accept Hanifiya and you will be safe.' Najran ended up paying the *jizya* protection money.

Whereas booty was the driving force behind the expansion of the cult, with success came diminishing opportunities for plunder; but with conquest came taxes that became an important source of revenue.

Christians and Jews who refused to convert paid the *jizya* in gold, silver, agricultural products or merchandise. Converts paid what was called a charity tax but in reality it ended up in the general fund and much of it went to pay for the costs of war. Gradually the balance of Hanifiya revenue shifted from plunder to tax. By then, top Hanifs such as ar-Rahman were among the richest people in the land.

After much of the north and central parts of Arabia were subjugated the Hanifs went south. A party of zealots first attacked at dawn a tribe in the mountainous region of what is now the Asir province of Saudi Arabia, slaying as many people as they could and making off with 150 camels, 3,000 goats and some women, and then attacked the commercial centre of the Asir region, an ancient caravan town named Jurash, in bizarre circumstances, for while the Hanifiya force was slaughtering the inhabitants of Jurash a delegation from the town was in Yathrib pledging allegiance to the Hanifiya. A raid deep into the heart of Yemen near Sana then followed, Hanifiya cavalry clashing with a local tribe and victorious after killing twenty of the tribesmen.

Punitive expeditions near the Syrian border in the north had aroused unease in the Byzantine empire, as Syria was a Byzantine province, and a few weeks after the raid into Yemen a rumour spread in Yathrib that Byzantine emperor Heraclius and his Christian Arab allies were equipping an army to attack the oasis, that he had given his soldiers a year's pay in advance in anticipation of a long campaign against the Hanifs and had commanded his feudatory border tribes to assemble to meet the Hanifiya challenge.

In response the Hanifiya leaders prepared an ambitious pre-emptive strike that involved marching 400 miles north to Syria across burning desert sands. Few of the lower-rank Hanifs wished to go on such an arduous expedition, aghast at the prospect of marching through a hot desert while being bellowed at by contemptuous officers, and then when they reached their destination, being heavily outnumbered in battle by Byzantine legions which had a formidable reputation. Also, it was the time of year when there was much ripe fruit that, if not eaten, would rot. A group of objectors assembled in a house to organise resistance to the campaign. A squad of zealots set fire to the house while the meeting was taking place. Only the owner of the house died in the flames, presumably because he could not bring himself to leave it, but others suffered broken bones jumping from the roof.

Still men begged to be exempted, alleging illness, poverty, family complications and many other excuses, including temptation into sin at the sight of Byzantine women, famed for their attractive fair skin and beguiling eyes. None of the excuses were accepted and, with violence taking place, backed up by threats of violence, joining the army for the duration of the expedition became a matter of survival. Al-Waqidi wrote that men 'chose security over fear'.

Armed men from outlying districts were also summoned, and they streamed into Yathrib from all directions. Some, especially the Bedouin contingents, lusted for adventure and the spoils of war, but most came unwillingly. In some of the districts, water was so precious that people rarely washed, and the men from those places were dirty and smelly. The whites of their eyes flashed in their sweaty faces, which the sun had burned black. Fiercely clannish, away from home, bored and for the most part not wishing to be there, they roamed the streets menacingly, on the lookout for perceived slights to their clan's honour. Criminal prisoners doing slave labour were also released so as to press them into service, and life in Yathrib became turbulent. The outsiders bivouacked in makeshift barracks, in the yards of which cooking fires blazed, and Yathrib resembled a garrison town or military encampment where fights raged in the streets and peaceful citizens locked themselves into their houses, remaining indoors shaking with fear. Street traders carried in their wares, barred the shutters and hired sturdy fellows with cudgels to guard their premises. Labour stopped in mills, offices and warehouses and the only workshops to remain operating were those of blacksmiths, from whose anvils came the ring of hammers forging arrowheads. Rich Hanifiya women donated gold bracelets and anklets and its top men responded generously to requests for gifts towards the fitting out of the expedition with weapons, camels, provisions and cash. A note has been preserved of a large amount of money that the merchant ar-Rahman contributed. He always spent a lot of time in the market making money, some of which he normally gave to his relations, but now he donated a hefty amount to the forthcoming campaign. Humbler believers delivered camel-loads of dates and grains. Neighbouring chiefs friendly to the Hanifs summoned their fellow tribesmen for the expedition. Those who summoned the tribes would also to a large extent be their leaders in battle. Just because a chief felt it expedient to be friendly towards the Hanifs, for whatever reason, did not mean all his tribe felt the same, and many tribesmen did not fancy this campaign at all.

When enough conscripts had been coerced into making their mark on the call-up papyrus, the force gathered at the place of departure, a mountain pass just north of Yathrib called Farewell Pass. According to al-Waqidi, it consisted of 30,000 men, 10,000 cavalry horses and more than 12,000 baggage camels.

From the pass the desert extended north in a murky reddish haze, the underworld, the playground of wicked genies. The reluctant conscripts must have gazed into it with loathing and apprehension. They were little more than fugitives, abducted to enter that underworld, not going of their own free will. Humans did not belong in that scorching sea of sand, the terrain a wasteland, in places strewn with occasional tortured, bush-like trees that crouched in the virulent sunlight, and elsewhere devoid of plants and dotted with stones, from where yellow dunes could be seen ahead. The conscripts must have thought with longing and regret of the lush fruit in their gardens and orchards falling to the ground in their absence to be devoured by insects and rodents.

The long column set out into the desert one morning at the beginning of October, which that year was not only not the slightest bit autumnal but was exceptionally hot, with a drought. The column took a caravan route, a road of sand beaten hard and level by centuries of use. Ancient milestones served as a comforting reminder of civilisation but nothing else, for they were so old the inscriptions had long ago worn away. Another trace of human concern for the coming and goings of travellers was the occasional clay tower to climb, primarily for a look around to see predators – highwaymen or wild animals. They could also be used as an escape if danger threatened.

By tradition, a remembrancer must have been hired to accompany the expedition, like war correspondents embedded with armies today.

Professional remembrancers had long been an important, honoured part of Arab culture. Up until then their chronicles had always been oral, often in the form of poetry, which was much admired. At this time, their chronicles started to be written down; and from translations of these, details of this particular Hanifiya expedition can be imagined.

Each man would have carried a small dusty round shield, poorly made of wood and iron, unable to turn aside thrusts; a sheathed sword on a belt; an unslung bow, and, on his back, a quiver of thirty arrows. Some also carried a spear but these were in short supply.

Remembrancers noted that most men wore a chainmail shirt between layers of clothing, covering it with linen to keep off the direct rays of the sun, preventing them from heating the bare metal to an unbearable condition. Their Byzantine opponents were so heavily armoured they were named *clibanarii*, from a Greek word for 'oven'. The Hanifiya army lacked a uniform. Remembrancers noted too that on these Hanifiya marches the warriors, though fallen in by companies while sergeants ran up and down the ranks yelling at them, always immediately mixed and merged as fellow tribesmen joined together, and this column must have streamed north in typical disorder, preceded by an advance squad of cavalry riding on ahead to scout and choose camping places for the troops, and followed by the baggage camels plodding along on their feet as wide as cushions to prevent sinking into soft sand. The force was unprofessional. Most of the men who had ever done any fighting at all were rustlers. Going on raids, called *razzias*, was a national sport.

No one could understand how this raw, rag-tag army dared challenge the Byzantines, but the men, at first, philosophically accepting their fate and making the best of it, marched fearlessly and determined, dreaming of the wealth of Syria that seemed theirs for the winning.

But then they began to feel the initial misgivings had been justified. The heat was terrific and water scarce. They started to suffer. The dry wind parched every face so that all the men had to constantly rub in oil; the dust choked, the sand fleas tormented. Two thirds of the force were infantry, and they trudged on, drenched in sweat, perpetually thirsty, fantasising about fair Byzantine women. An increasing number grew footsore and dropped out by the roadside, unable to rise despite the sergeants' kicks. At midday it was no longer the sun alone that persecuted from above – the entire sky was like a metal dome grown white with heat. The merciless light pushed down from all directions; the sun was the whole sky, impossible to travel under, so that the men travelled at night, resting during the day in the shade provided by the shadow of a reclining camel. Amid gravel and cursed stones, between boulders, over stretches of loamy sand and parched plains with sparse thickets of scrub tamarisk, they entered the empty desolation of the region that merged into Syria, reaching a minor oasis called Tabuk that was only seventy miles from the Syrian border – but, dehydrated and utterly exhausted, simply could go no further. And even if they could, the infantry would be in no condition to fight.

By now, it was not only the plodding camels that had the hump. The men were angry that because of the commanders' foolish obstinacy they were parched and knackered and were to be slain by Byzantines. But, with scouts and spies reporting there was no sign anywhere of any Byzantine army (the rumours had been false), food running short and available water inadequate, the commanders reluctantly decided the column had to turn back. When they announced their decision the men would have cheered if their throats were not so dry with the acrid dust. After three weeks the disgruntled force departed the way it had come. As well as not encountering a single Yellow Skin, as the Byzantines were called, nothing had been acquired in plunder, and fair women remained just a sexual fantasy. Before leaving, treaties were made with nearby Christian and Jewish tribes that included the usual extortion of protection money. Khalid stayed behind with 420 cavalrymen, leading them on a raid to the north-east, where they subdued an important defiant Christian tribe, taking prisoner its chief whom they surprised when he was out hunting, thus securing the surrender of the stronghold. The defeated tribe had to make an immediate payment of 2,000 camels, 800 slaves, 400 coats of mail and 400 lances, while, as from the following year, for its own security, to prevent such a thing happening again, all the tribe's men were to make a hefty annual payment of *jizya*.

Though the aborted expedition to Syria failed, it showed that the Hanifs now felt they could challenge the Byzantine empire, an astonishing presumption. It also revealed to them the demanding logistics required for ambitious campaigns, the problems when provisioning a big army over long distances, knowledge that was soon to come in useful.

And the impressive show of military strength consolidated the submission of the whole of western Arabia, down the entire Red Sea coast from the Gulf of Aqaba to Aden. So many southern tribes sent envoys to Yathrib that the year was called 'the year of deputations' and Hanifiya officials became accustomed to southern accents.

After attacks on important northern tribes had ended with all accepting Hanifiya suzerainty, now in the south Hanifs destroyed the temple of Dhu Khalasa, the male equivalent of al-Lat, the destination of the annual pilgrimage for many southern Arabs. The Hanifs slew 300 men who rushed to defend their beloved temple.

Hanifiya administrators and tax collectors now swarmed over the entire west of the peninsula. In the south the progress of Hanifiya was bound up with successful intervention in local quarrels, while to the north the Hanifs' attention was increasingly directed to the strategic importance of Syria.

Agreements were made with Christian tribes in the south of Syria, the most important being that of Ayla. The tribute for Ayla was fixed at 300 gold dinars annually. Near Ayla territory was a fishing town inhabited by Jews, who were required to pay to the Hanifs annually a quarter of their produce of fish, fruit and yarn.

At first the Hanifs were prepared to form alliances with Christian tribes in Syria but this policy was changed to waging war on them until they paid the *jizya*. If they refused, or displayed any other sign of hostility, they were enslaved or slain in a succession of punitive expeditions.

On one of these expeditions the Hanifs were surprised by a vastly superior combined force of Byzantines and Arabs gathered by Heraclius. The Hanifs charged into battle anyway, on the basis that they welcomed either outcome, victory or martyrdom. Their commander, Zayd, was slain; then the second-in-command, a young man named Jafar, aged only 33, also fell, both his arms chopped off; and then the third-in-command, Rawaha, was killed as well. Khalid was then handed the Hanifiya standard, which was originally white but was now dyed red with the blood of the three slain leaders who had been carrying it, and organised an orderly retreat that entailed the main force fleeing through a narrow mountain pass while a sacrificial rearguard held off an overwhelming enemy like the 300 Spartans at Thermopylae.

But in time these expeditions achieved their purpose and throughout Arabia religious domination was reinforced with social organisation. Tribesmen came as envoys from all over the peninsula, many of them not understanding the implications of the religious aspect. To them, being friendly with this new powerful tribe was purely political expediency, a misunderstanding that was to have serious consequences. From 632 rebellions spread throughout Arabia. Though not religious from the rebels' point of view, Hanifs called the suppression of the revolts the Wars of Apostasy. Military campaigns combated and defeated the many tribes that the Hanifs considered apostates. The Hanifs' view was that most of the nomad Arabian tribes had converted to their religion. But many tribes that the Hanifs presumed to have converted had not shared that presumption. They felt that the most they could be accused of was political disloyalty. The nomads in particular saw nothing to gain in abandoning their casual way of life for the constant rituals and obligations of this new, demanding religion, and had not so much converted as judiciously become friendly with the new most powerful tribe, common practice in the lawless, anarchic land.

But Hanifs did not regard this traditional behaviour as valid in their case, because they were special. Hanifiya was a new sort of tribe, one based not on blood-relationship but on a common religious allegiance. The old rules did not apply. Always before, the issue was purely what was politically expedient; now Hanifiya had introduced religion. Hanifs claimed they alone represented divine will in politics. The Bedouin did not understand the significance of this claim.

Also, within each tribe there were smaller groups intensely jealous of each other, and usually pursuing contrary policies. A deputation from a tribe going to the Hanifs usually represented only one faction in the tribe and often no one but themselves. That a 'deputation' came from a certain tribe and converted to Hanifiya did not mean the whole of that tribe became Hanifs.

One tragic case of misunderstanding was that of the 'deputation' from the big Christian tribe of Ghassan along the Syrian border, which actively opposed Hanifiya and whose territory acted as a buffer zone for Byzantium. This story is evidence that despite the supposed envoys Ghassan showed no signs of accepting Hanifiya. It had been the act of one of their chiefs, who intercepted and executed a leading Hanif, a scarred survivor of many battles who was carrying a letter to the governor of a south Syrian city, that led to the battle in which the young Hanifiya second-in-command, Jafar, was slain. Such an act could not be allowed to go unpunished, despite the risk that the Ghassanids might be able to persuade Heraclius's representative in Damascus to send them troops, which indeed was what happened. Their chiefs had for a long time been on friendly terms with the Byzantines and in return for a subsidy had defended the Byzantine frontier from the nomads. In the rumour that Heraclius had mustered Arab tribes on the Syrian border for a long campaign against the Hanifs that never materialised, Ghassan had been one of the four tribes mentioned.

In that atmosphere, three members of the tribe went to the Hanifs, who convinced them that Hanifiya was the only true religion but then went home and did nothing about it. The Ghassanids continued to oppose Hanifiya. Thus the Hanifs failed to win the hostile Christian tribe over to their side, despite the three men who claimed to represent it implying that it now supported Hanifiya. The Ghassanids paid heavily for this misunderstanding. They were one of the many tribes to suffer in the Wars of Apostasy.

In an exchange of letters with the Ghassanids the Hanifs promised protection to those who had clearly converted and warned those 'who go back from their religion' that they forfeit this protection. The Ghassanids replied that they had never converted in the first place. This was dismissed on the evidence in the Hanifiya records of their 'deputation' accepting Hanifiya on their behalf. They wrote back that they objected to the contributions they were expected to make to Hanifiya, whether in money or in kind, adding, 'We never sent anyone to represent us.'

Apart from this exchange of letters, the three false delegates, two of whom had since died, and a few Ghassanid tribesmen who had joined the Byzantine troops in the battle against a Hanif force in which Jafar fell, no one in the tribe had had any previous contact with Hanifiya. The first Hanifs they ever saw were cavalry charging them with drawn swords. This was also the last thing that many of them ever saw.

Khalid was active in these murderous campaigns. According to fifteenth-century historian Hafiz ibn al-Hajar, he burned alive or decapitated many tribesmen, once beheading an alleged apostate, raping the man's beautiful wife and then setting the severed head on fire in order to cook his dinner on it. Some say that Khalid knew that the man was not an apostate but accused him of it because he fancied the beautiful wife.

With Khalid mercilessly rampaging around the peninsula with his cavalry, within a year the Hanifs, through slaughter and terror, massacres and threats, imposed the authority of Hanifiya on all the unwilling Bedouin tribes. Following the precedent of the bloody Wars of Apostasy, all Hanifs agreed that a sane male apostate must be killed but there was disagreement on whether a female apostate should be put to death or held under house arrest *ad infinitum*.

Khalid was given the mission of destroying the forces of one of the most powerful of the rebel tribes. During a week-long siege of the tribe's fortified town of Yamama in east-central Arabia, he launched a series of attacks along the entire front. Dreadful carnage took place in a gulley in which blood ran in a rivulet down to a *wadi*. As a result, this gulley was called ever afterwards the Gulley of Blood.

Following the carnage only 7,000 rebels, a quarter of the tribe's army, remained in fighting shape, and they retreated to a walled garden of the town and barred the gate with a heavy plank at chest height. A strong attacking soldier, Al-Bara ibn Malik, climbed the wall, jumped into the garden, killed the guards and, lifting the plank, opened the gate. As the attackers stormed into the garden the defenders fell back, the tribe's leader, Musaylima bin Habib, joining them with no intention of surrendering. He was slain but no one knew who killed him, for he was struck simultaneously by a javelin in the stomach and an arrow in the back and while lying on the ground was decapitated, possibly while still alive.

The slaying of Musaylima was followed by the rout and massacre of his men, and the garden became known as the Garden of Death.

After crushing all the rebellions within a year, Hanifiya armies marched north to Palestine and Syria and, under Khalid, now using Yamama as his base, to the Sassanid Persian empire's province of Asoristan, the political and economic centre of the Sassanid state. Khalid embarked on a six-month rampage in what is now western Iraq, defeating the Persians and their Christian Arab allies in numerous clashes. These were bloody battles. Thirty thousand Persian and Christian Arab soldiers were killed in one battle, 70,000 in another. In the latter, thousands of captured soldiers were brought to the edge of a river, where they were decapitated. Their bodies were thrown in the river, causing it to flow red for three days.

A Byzantine counter-offensive threatened the forces of Arab leaders in Palestine, and Khalid was ordered to take his men to Syria as reinforcement. He probably began his march to Syria in early April 634.

A stretch of the march necessitated him and his men, numbering up to 800, trekking across an arid desert for six days until reaching a source of water at a place called Suwa. Beyond the Euphrates to the south the vague sandy road that led to Suwa passed through an utterly inhospitable world, and before travellers came to Suwa's wells and nourishing fields there lay a profoundly doleful underworld, an accursed, dangerous and horrid expanse, a dismal desert that allowed for no dallying, even if not dashing to the aid of beleaguered colleagues.

As Khalid's men did not have enough waterskins to traverse this dismal land with their horses and camels, before setting out he let twenty of his camels drink a lot of water and then sealed their mouths so they were unable to eat and thereby spoil the water in their stomachs. He had some of these camels slaughtered on every day of the desert march so that his men could drink the water stored in the stomach of the carcase.

For six days the force moved patiently across the desert, the vanguard following Khalid and the bell of the lead camel, and the rest following the vanguard, just like any of the long caravans that traversed the region, only carrying not goods but weapons. It passed through a jumble of ghastly sandstone boulders, grotesque and up-thrust masses that glistened with the blackness of ore instead of stone, a gloomy sheen that made them resemble a towering town of iron. For six days the soldiers' world was a world damned beyond all reckoning, filled with pale sand to a far horizon pallid with heat. They crossed dunes, down whose backs the wind had evidently left repulsively dainty waves and folds. Bleached bones often lay along the way, the rib cage and thigh bone of a camel or desiccated human limbs jutting up out of the waxy dust. The men blinked as they passed, and went on nourishing their hope. By the sixth day they were out of danger, had reached Suwa, and escaped the wasteland's horrors.

This desert march has become legendary. Afterwards Khalid's fame was so illustrious that people told stories of him as they used to tell stories of their gods before the Hanifs banned the veneration of these gods. Arab sources marvelled at Khalid's endurance, while modern scholars have seen him as a master of strategy, renowned Israeli historian Moshe Gil calling the march 'a feat that has no parallel' and a testament to Khalid's qualities as an outstanding commander.

The arrival of Khalid's force, though small, galvanised the Arab invaders, who immediately embarked on a renewed ferocious assault on Syria, a cruel, merciless invasion in which many Syrians perished. Every territory the Hanifs conquered they plundered, and enormous wealth flowed back to Yathrib. Deserted villages were laid waste, gardens ravished of their fruit trees. The Hanifs left behind them towns in which the cries of the wounded mingled with those of the women as they were dragged away by the warriors, who cast lots for them; charred, plundered houses; and mutilated corpses, some of them grotesquely vertical at the side of the road, impaled.

Arab operations culminated in the submission of Palmyra in central Syria and three victorious battles on the west coast. After the Arabs had conquered most of the Syrian countryside, in 635 Khalid, by then a general, captured Damascus following a failed attempt by the Arabs the previous year. With the Arabs also laying siege to Jerusalem, the alarmed Byzantines tried to regain control. They fielded a much bigger army, advancing into southern Syria in the spring of 636. Khalid withdrew his forces from Damascus to prepare for renewed confrontation, which came at a six-day battle by the Yarmuk river, along what are now the borders of Syria-Jordan and Syria-Israel, east of the Sea of Galilee, near the Arabian peninsula.

It was one of the most decisive battles of history. The Arabs annihilated the Byzantine troops, slaying more than 50,000. Some accounts say the defeat came because the Byzantines ran out of arrows, while others say it was because Khalid took advantage of a sandstorm to charge the Byzantine troops as they were blinded by the sand blown full in their faces. Anticipating victory, the previous day he had sent a force of cavalry to a bridge to block the Byzantine soldiers' retreat. The river flowed at the foot of steep slopes, and many jumped from the cliffs and were smashed on the rocks below, some mistakenly believing they could escape in the waters and others committing suicide. Others were slain as they fled.

Khalid then recaptured Damascus.

The whole of the Byzantine empire was now vulnerable. Jerusalem, where many of the survivors of the disaster at Yarmuk, most of them cavalrymen who had left the infantry to their fate, had taken shelter, surrendered, but Patriarch Sophronius, who came from Damascus, put off the inevitable by insisting he would only hand over the keys of the city to the Arab chief, Umar, in person. Khalid was sent pretending to be Umar because he looked like him but was recognised and eventually Umar came and rode into the Christian holy city on a striking albino camel.

A 17,000-strong army of Arabs then conquered the whole of northern Syria and Anatolia (roughly modern Turkey). In Anatolia an advance force of the invaders, élite light cavalry led by Khalid personally, was riding on to Antioch when it nearly captured Heraclius, who had just fled the city for his capital, Constantinople. To escape, Heraclius had to hastily take a mountain path. In Constantinople, as well as being mortally ill, he wasted his time in self-indulgence and a sectarian Christian dispute and the Arabs won from him nearly all he had gained from the Persians in the prolonged conflict that had fatally weakened both empires. The Arabs, as well as benefiting from the conflict also gained from the dispute, which was so bitter eastern provinces of

Byzantium were estranged from Constantinople and gave no support to the imperial armies.

When Khalid's cavalry reached Antioch the Greek troops who manned it sallied out hoping to destroy it before it was joined by the main Arab army but at the river Orontes they lost the major Battle of the Iron Bridge twelve miles from the city, which the Arabs then besieged. It surrendered with the terms that all the surviving Greek troops would be given safe passage to Constantinople. On this occasion the Arabs untypically kept their promise.

Khalid took part in more than a hundred fights, ranging from major battles to skirmishes and single combat. On his deathbed five years after the Battle of the Iron Bridge he said, 'I have fought in so many battles seeking martyrdom that there is no spot in my body left without a scar or a wound. And yet here I am, dying on my bed like an old camel.'

Following the conquest of Syria, other lands were swiftly subjugated – at the expense of the Arabs' homeland. The booty, land, slaves and share of *jizya* up for grabs in the campaigns of conquest were so great that tribesmen from all over Arabia joined the Hanifiya forces, adventurers taking with them their families and flocks, which depopulated the peninsula, so that vital complex irrigation systems were neglected, causing erosion of fertile soil.

In 641 a battle at Nahavand in the Persian Highlands between Arab and Persian forces ended in disastrous defeat for the Persians, paving the way for the Arab conquest nine years later that led to the collapse of the Persians' great Sassanid empire. At Nahavand 30,000 Arab troops attacked a Persian army of 150,000 men that was entrenched in a strong fortified position. After an indecisive skirmish, the Arabs deceived them with the false rumour that Umar had died, and withdrew from the battlefield. The Persians, full of confidence, made a major tactical error by abandoning their position to mount an ill-prepared pursuit of the Arabs, who retreated to a safe area and eventually surrounded and trapped them in a narrow valley. The Persian army was massacred, their dead said to number 100,000.

Another Arab army, during an invasion of the Byzantine province of Egypt, defeated the Byzantines at a battle near Heliopolis, then, after a siege, captured the beautiful town of Alexandria on the Mediterranean coast that had replaced Athens as the main centre of philosophical thought. Arab general Amr ibn al-As asked Umar what to do about Alexandria's prestigious library and Umar replied, 'Destroy it.' Amr dutifully had all the books and scrolls burnt in the furnaces of the city's numerous bath-houses.

Amr then demolished the city walls and made his headquarters at a strategic location near the Nile delta, a settlement named Fustat, which he used as a base for further westward expansion, his troops and their families turning it into a garrison town. The following year he built the first mosque in Egypt, named after him, at the site he had pitched his tent on arrival. In a treaty signed with the Byzantine governor of Egypt, he guaranteed the security of Egypt's population if all non-Muslim men paid the *jizya* tax.

Luck had been with the invaders, for as well as the long war between Byzantium and Persia that began as competition over who should control the petty monarchs of the Caucasus and continued for dominion over the Fertile Crescent that had exhausted both of these formerly mighty empires, the region, which in the previous century had experienced the world's first pandemic of the *Yersinia pestis* plague, had recently suffered a second outbreak.

The new outbreak of plague had infected the whole region; yet just as many people escaped as had the misfortune to succumb, either because they escaped the infection altogether or because they recovered if they happened to be infected. But not a single person in the entire region could escape the Hanifs: no one was completely untouched. Some were killed without any justification; others were enslaved. Those who surrendered with the promise of mercy after they had put up resistance were massacred, the Hanifs, following their custom, making no attempt to honour their pledges to non-believers. The Hanifs then drove westward along the north African coast, inflicting a disastrous defeat on Carthage; northward, invading countries of the Caucasus; and in 633 had invaded Persia. Three years later they won the Battle of al-Kadisiya, slaying most of the defending commanders, near the Sassanid capital Ctesiphon.

The Sassanid survivors of al-Kadisiya later regrouped and fought the Arabs again in several battles, all of which they lost. After two of the defeats the Sassanid commander, an aristocrat named Hormuzan who was the governor of Khuzestan, one of the richest provinces of the Sassanid empire, agreed to pay tribute in return for peace, and each time he reneged on the agreement, stopping the payment of the tribute. As a result he clashed with the Arabs yet again, and again was defeated, after which the towns of Khuzestan were seized one by one. Hormuzan fled but was defeated near the city of Shushtar, which cost the lives of 900 of his men, while 600 were captured and would later be executed. Nevertheless, he managed to reach Shushtar, which the Arabs then besieged.

Shushtar, surrounded by rivers and canals, was well fortified but was anyway captured. Several different versions tell of how, all involving some form of treachery. Hormuzan retreated to the citadel and continued his resistance. The surviving men in the citadel with him killed their own family members and threw their property into a river rather than let the Arabs have it as plunder. Hormuzan was forced to surrender and was taken by the Arabs to Yathrib, which now, due to a great increase in population and dwellings was commonly called Medina, 'the city'.

Nineteenth-century British scholar, historian and Christian theologian George Rawlinson wrote that Hormuzan, on obtaining an audience with Umar, said he was thirsty and asked for a cup of water, which was given him; he then looked suspiciously around, as if expecting to be stabbed while drinking. 'Fear nothing,' said Umar. 'Your life is safe till you have drunk the water.' Hormuzan craftily flung the cup to the ground, and Umar felt that he had been outwitted but that he must keep his word.

Umar would have been wiser not to be so honourable, for Hormuzan then led a successful plot to assassinate him. In 644 a disgruntled Persian slave, a soldier captured at the Battle of Nahavand, stabbed Umar several times in the stomach during dawn prayers and then committed suicide. Umar lived for three days before dying of dehydration. He was unable to take liquids, which poured out of him through his wounds. Umar's son, Ubaidallah, slew Hormuzan in revenge. The new chief, Uthman, instead of punishing Ubaidallah, had him pardoned. Hormuzan supporters protested to Uthman in vain and so tried to slay Ubaidallah, who had to flee.

A new Byzantine emperor, Constans the Second, was determined to retake Alexandria, and, having been reliably informed it was weakly defended, sent a fleet carrying troops across the Mediterranean. This fleet crossed the sea unopposed and took the city in a surprise amphibious attack. The Byzantines then advanced down the east bank of the Nile, meeting in battle an Arab army led by Amr near the small town of Nikiou. Byzantine archers shot at the Arab cavalry regiment closest to the river from flanking ships cleverly deployed to sail parallel to the marching army. Amr's horse was killed under him. This was followed by hand-to-hand fighting that Arabs usually relished and excelled at, but on this occasion the regiment that had borne the brunt of the rain of arrows fired from the ships was now demoralised and broke and ran, and Amr ordered the retreat of his whole army.

Arab morale was renewed by the success of their *mubarizun*, 'duellist' or 'champion', in single combat with a Byzantine champion who strode out from the Byzantine ranks in golden armour into the no man's land separating the two forces with a challenge. Such duels were an ancient custom in the region, hence the story in the Bible of David and Goliath. The *mubarizun*, though he slew his gold-plated adversary, was himself mortally wounded. Another grinding mêlée followed, in which the Arabs prevailed, and the Byzantine force retreated in disarray, back to Alexandria, which eventually fell to the pursuing Arabs, who stormed it, regaining the city.

Up until then the Arabs had lacked naval power. Uthman, though aged 70 and devoid of military experience, having been a merchant, noting how the Byzantines had crossed the Mediterranean unopposed, quickly built a war fleet. Defence was never its main role however, but sea-borne aggression. Its first target was Cyprus, one of Byzantium's chief naval bases. The Cypriot capital, Constantia, was sacked, its harbour installations destroyed, the surrounding countryside ravaged. The Arabs then attacked Sicily, managing to escape back to Syria with a huge trove of pillaged riches stripped from churches and the homes of the inhabitants. In 654 they launched a still more formidable expedition that captured the Greek island of Rhodes. The following year a Byzantine fleet engaged in the first of a whole millennium of sea fights between Christians and Arabs. It was catastrophic. The Byzantine navy was shattered, the emperor himself escaping only by disguising himself by changing clothes with one of his men.

Discontent with Uthman mounted in 656 over the favour he showed to his own family, who enjoyed a monopoly of influential and lucrative appointments. He was at home when armed men from Egypt arrived and demanded the dismissal of one of them, the Egyptian governor, which he pretended to grant. But on their way back to Egypt they caught an African slave carrying a message from him to the governor with orders for their execution. They returned, stoned Uthman and then stabbed him to death in his house.

The next chief, Ali, who had been excluded from government during the leadership of Umar, was assassinated in 661 at the instigation of the governor of Syria, Muawiya, who had opposed him, causing an Arab civil war. The two had led their armies to a stalemate at a battle in 657. After the murder, Muawiya gained recognition as chief by his Syrian supporters and his ally Amr, who conquered Egypt from Ali's governor. Muawiya moved his capital to Damascus and founded the Umayyad dynasty. In 669 the Arabs again invaded Sicily, naming the seaweed-scented port their 200 warships landed at *Mars el-Allah*, 'Harbour of God', which became Marsala, later best known for its production of fortified wine.

Muawiya engaged his troops in almost annual land and sea raids against the Byzantines and, in 674, backed by ships carrying heavy siege engines and huge catapults, they besieged Constantinople. But the Byzantine fortifications withstood the assaults and, moreover, the defenders had a secret weapon. To this day no one knows the composition of 'Greek fire'. A prototype of the modern flame-thrower, it was apparently based on a mixture of sulphur, naphtha and quicklime that burst explosively into flames when wetted. Sprayed over an enemy ship or poured into long cartridges and catapulted against its objective, the flaming, oil-based liquid floated on the surface of the sea, often igniting the wooden hulls of the ships and causing an additional hazard to those who tried to jump overboard. After five years of this the charred remnants of the Arab fleet returned home.

Chapter 2

Ukba rides into the Atlantic; Musa conquers Spain; the reigns of al-Mansur, Harun Rashid, al-Mutasim; *mamlukes*; *takiya*; the devastation of India; Alp Arslan; the Battle of Didgori

In 691, or 692, Arabs finished building the Dome of the Rock shrine in Jerusalem. An inscription inside is the first extant use of the word 'Islam', which means 'Submission to Allah'. And throughout that decade the practitioners of this religion came increasingly to be referred to as Muslims, 'those who submit', though 'Hanifiya' and 'Hanifs' remained in common usage for many more decades. The earliest versions of the *Koran* had 'Hanifiya' and 'Hanifs': 'Islam' and 'Muslims' are later substitutions. The most glaring example is that in 3:19 of the current *Koran*. The cult was not called Islam until decades after its foundation, and the sentence in 3:19, 'The only true faith in Allah's sight is Islam' instead of 'Islam' originally had 'Hanifiya', written by an early convert named Ibn Masud.

Uthman had established an official version of the *Koran* but six other versions still circulated for several centuries, despite his attempt to have all copies of them burnt. Koranic commentators continued quoting from earlier versions, and in the ninth century Muslims complained about the use of Ibn Masud's version, indicating that at least his version still circulated; and four centuries after that a Christian writing in Egypt can still refer to the time when 'the Hanifite nation appeared and humbled the Romans'.

This commentator noted the astonishing speed of the Arabs' expansion. By 711 Arab armies were simultaneously invading India and Spain. 'The Hanifite nation' had 'humbled the Romans' within a decade; in that short space of time the Arabs had conquered Egypt and Armenia; in another ten years, they had conquered the Persian Sassanid empire and the entire coast of north Africa, where Arab general Ukba took the message of Islam with such missionary zeal that he spurred his horse into the Atlantic surf. A contemporary chronicler wrote that Ukba said, 'O Allah, if the sea had not prevented me, I would have galloped on for ever like Alexander the Great, upholding your faith and fighting the unbelievers!', while historian Edward Gibbon wrote that Ukba exclaimed, 'If my course were not stopped by this sea, I would still go on, to the unknown kingdoms of the West, preaching the unity of the holy name, and putting to the sword the rebellious nations who worship gods other than Allah.'

With an ocean on the west and deserts in the south, the Muslims went north. From Morocco, Arab general Musa sent a force of 7,000 warriors, mostly Berbers, who were Saharan nomads, under a Muslim Berber named Tariq, to Spain, with a stop on Gibraltar, whose name commemorates the landing: *Jabel el Tariq* – the Mountain of Tariq. Musa then came with reinforcements, taking the command from Tariq, and over the next few years many more Muslim warriors joined him, subduing key cities. The Visigothic capital of Toledo in central Spain was captured without opposition. By 716 southern Spain, named by the Muslims Al-Andalus, today's Andalusia, had emerged as the first European province of their empire, and Musa completed the conquest of Spain except for an isolated independent Christian enclave in the Asturias mountains in the extreme north.

The conquest led by Musa was a brutal, horrifying event, the Spanish subjugated through violent and ferocious warfare. Many were enslaved or simply murdered. The conquerors raped traumatised women on the very day the men had slain their families.

The *Chronicle of 754* says:

> Musa invaded Spain to destroy it. After forcing his way to Toledo, the royal city, he imposed on the adjacent regions an evil and fraudulent peace. He decapitated on a scaffold those noble lords

who had stayed. The ancient and once flourishing city of Zaragoza was now openly exposed to sword, famine and captivity. He ruined beautiful cities, burning them with fire; condemned lords and powerful men to the cross; and butchered youths and infants.

Roger Collins wrote in his 2014 book *Caliphs and Kings: Spain, 796-1031*, 'The conquest of Spain put especial emphasis upon destruction and the display of dead enemies, with a lively slave trade as an additional incentive.'

The Muslim army then crossed the Pyrenees and approached Paris.

Here, at last, in 732, it was stopped, beaten by a little army of rugged Frankish warriors in a battle regarded as one of the world's pivotal moments. The *Chronicle of 754* recorded that, 'The men of the north stood as motionless as a wall; they were like a belt of ice frozen together, and not to be dissolved, as they slew the Arabs with the sword.'

The Muslim army in fact was comprised mostly of Berbers and other Moors. It was almost entirely light cavalry, with simple, basic stuffed cloth saddles. The Franks had a small contingent of heavy cavalry. But it was too heavy. This was the first battle in which cavalrymen fought in full armour. They could do so because of the invention of the Norman saddle. But they were not used to this innovation and were clumsy, so when the commander, Charles, duke and prince of the Franks, saw that the Muslims were preparing for a full-scale attack he ordered them to dismount and fight in the ranks of the foot soldiers. The Muslims could not break through despite numerous attempts and retired in order to try and save the enormous amount of plunder they had collected on their march. But they could not even do this and panicked and fled without it, their leader slain in the retreat. Gibbon wrote that Charles was 'the hero of the age', adding, 'Had the Muslims won, their fleet might have sailed without a naval combat into the mouth of the Thames'. For ending Muslim ambitions in the north, Charles earned himself the name of Martel, the Hammer. The Muslims withdrew south of the Pyrenees in 759.

By then they ruled an empire stretching from the Atlantic to north India. They believed that they were fulfilling a divine plan and that if slain in battle they would go to heaven. These beliefs made them formidable enemies. One wrote, 'We went to meet them with small abilities and weak forces, and Allah made us triumph, and gave us possession of their territories.'

Determined to eliminate Christianity, they issued a series of edicts requiring the destruction of every cross in Egypt; in 709 they captured the key Byzantine stronghold of Tyana in Cappadocia, its inhabitants taking refuge in the deserts whose contorted outcrops of soft and friable tufa offered troglodytic sanctuary; and in 717 they made another attempt to take Constantinople, besieging it with a huge army, again backed by a fleet of ships. This blockade continued throughout the harshest winter in living memory, with the besiegers having no protection but their flimsy tents. Soon they were also reduced to eating their camels, horses and donkeys and even cannibalism. Famine inevitably fetched disease, with the frozen ground making burial impossible. Greek fire meanwhile again exacted a daily toll among the ships. A Bulgarian army delivered the final blow, falling on the diseased and demoralised Muslims after marching down from the north in the spring. What remained of the Muslim army dragged itself back to Syria; but of the fleet, now dangerously unseaworthy, only five ships reached home.

Muslims repeatedly raided Sardinia and, in 721, to save from desecration the remains of St Augustine of Hippo, the early fifth-century Christian writer from Roman north Africa whose *On Christian Doctrine* revolutionised the way in which the Christian scripture was interpreted and understood, King Liutprand of Lombardy sent envoys to ransom them at great cost, and they were re-interred in his capital, Pavia. By 730 Muslim troops had extended Islam to the southernmost region of mainland Portugal, 'the west', *al-Gharb*, the Algarve.

As well as unrelentingly attacking other lands across the known accessible world, the Muslims constantly warred among themselves in bloodthirsty conflicts. Umayyad rule in the Middle East ended after seven years of regional revolts, religious disputes and confusingly intertwined dynastic struggles that included civil war.

The last Umayyad caliph, Marwan the Second, arrested the head of the rival Abbasid family, Ibrahim, who died in captivity, probably murdered. The Abbasid family fled to Kufa in Khorsan, an area where lived non-Arab Muslims who were influenced by Abbasid propaganda. Khorasanian rebel leaders pledged allegiance to Ibrahim's brother, Abul Abbas, called 'the Blood-shedder' for his ruthless tactics and to instil fear in his enemies.

After a decisive Umayyad defeat on a cold January day in 750 in a battle by the Greater Zab river in what is now Iraq, Marwan escaped the battlefield and fled to a small town in the Nile delta where a few months later he was slain in a short unequal fight that was little more than an assassination. The victors of the Battle of the Greater Zab systematically massacred most of the entire extended Umayyad family to become the Abbasid caliphate. A few Umayyads who remained alive, mortally wounded, were laid on the floor side by side, covered by a carpet, and used as a banqueting table by honoured guests of the gloating Abbasids. 'And those who were present at the scene,' it was said, 'ate while the death-rattle still sounded in the throats of the expiring victims.'

Abul Abbas's brother, Abu Jafar, led an army to Iraq where he received a submission from the Umayyad governor after informing him of Marwan's death. The governor had taken refuge in a garrison town. He was promised a safe-conduct by Abu Jafar and Abul Abbas but after he surrendered they had him executed along with some of his followers.

Soon the Abbasid caliphate was firmly in control, the empire to which it succeeded the main civilisation west of China.

Abul Abbas died of smallpox in June 754 to be succeeded by the equally cruel and treacherous Abu Jafar, who adopted the title al-Mansur, 'the Victorious', and ten years later founded Baghdad at the same time as slaying an uncle who had challenged his right to the throne. And he carefully planned the assassination of an army general whose popularity he feared. The general was conversing with him when, at an appointed signal, al-Mansur's guards rushed in and inflicted mortal wounds. John Aikin, author of biographical and critical essays and prefaces, in his ten-volume *General Biography* of 1800, wrote that al-Mansur, not content with the assassination, 'committed outrages on the dead body, and kept it several days in order to glut his eyes with the spectacle'.

Aikin added that al-Mansur's treatment of his Christian subjects was severe: 'He collected from them capitation [the *jizya* poll tax] with much vigour and impressed upon them marks of slavery.'

In 763 al-Mansur sent troops to conquer Al-Andalus, the remaining province of the Umayyad caliphate then at its greatest extent, comprising most of Iberia and part of southern France. A survivor of the Abbasid massacre of the Umayyads, Abd al-Rahman, after being on the run for five years, several times dramatically avoiding capture closely, had soon, with enormous bloodshed, founded a new Umayyad dynasty in Spain, as emir of Cordoba controlling all of Al-Andalus.

Al-Rahman, heavily outnumbered by the attacking Abbasid army, barricaded himself in a fortress. After a long and gruelling siege it seemed as if he was about to be beaten but he made a desperate sortie with his much smaller force, charging the resting Abbasid troops and crushing them. He sent the Abbasid governor's head to al-Mansur, who, it is said, exclaimed, 'Allah be praised for putting a sea between me and Abd al-Rahman.' After that, the chastened al-Mansur withdrew from Al-Andalus, concentrating on holding the eastern part of his empire on lands that were once part of Persia and continuing the Muslim assaults on Byzantium, constantly invading its eastern provinces.

He died in 775, the same year as Byzantine emperor Constantine, who was known by the unattractive epithet of Copronymus, meaning Named Turd. According to legend, this was because as a baby he did a poo in the baptismal font just as the priest was pronouncing his name, but it is more likely he was given such an ugly nickname due to unpopularity. He was openly bisexual, and filled his court with effeminate rouged youths. Despite this proclivity, Constantine the Turd was married thrice, fathering six sons, one of whom on his death assumed the throne as Leo the Fourth.

Leo IV died five years later of a high fever caused by tuberculosis after successfully repelling an attack by the Abbasids against Asia Minor.

This success of the Byzantine empire deterred the Muslims from further aggression for a couple of decades, but then they mounted a military expedition against it – led by a boy of 14. And a few years later this precocious adolescent led another invasion, this time a huge undertaking that even reached the outskirts of Constantinople on the Asian side of the Bosporus. According to contemporary Muslim chronicler al-Tabari, the invaders slew tens of thousands of Byzantine soldiers during this campaign and needed 20,000 mules to cart home the booty.

This youth, Harun Rashid, was a son of Caliph Mahdi and when Mahdi died Rashid's older brother Hadi assumed the throne, with Rashid fully expecting to be next in line. But Hadi made his own infant son crown prince instead of Rashid. Inevitably Hadi then died suddenly in mysterious and suspicious circumstances and Rashid was proclaimed caliph.

Outside the Islamic world Rashid is the most famous caliph, known for being the ruler in the voyages of Sindbad in the *Thousand and One Nights* and portrayed in two of the other tales as a benevolent monarch. His reign is traditionally regarded as the beginning of the Islamic golden age, an age when the prestige of learning was highly prized. The flawless recitation of an appropriate verse or entire ode at the court of a caliph could bring hefty rewards – not only a magnificent robe of honour but serious cash as well.

The splendid opulence of the luxury at these courts was funded by conquest, by revenues from subjugated lands, by booty, slavery, annual tribute and the *jizya* poll tax. In reality Rashid was ruthless and rapacious. When his forces yet again invaded Byzantium's eastern provinces in 791 he exacted a shameful peace, involving a tribute that the Byzantines could ill afford, as vast areas of its empire had become desperately underpopulated by an outbreak of plague.

And his successors were no more peaceful. Rashid died in 809, aged only 43. Three years later an invasion force of his successor, Amin, ravaged the Tyrrhenian Sea islands of Ponza and Ischia and conquered the island of Lampedusa, only seventy miles away from Abbasid-held Tunisia, facilitating raids on Sicily.

Arabs had first attacked Sicily in 728. This attack failed but twelve years later an Arab expedition from Tunisia captured Syracuse. While preparing to conquer all of Sicily from that base, however, the Arabs had to abandon it to return to Tunisia to deal with a Berber revolt. A third attack in 752 aimed only to sack the southern port again. Another Arab force was sent from north Africa to conquer Sicily in 812, breaking a ten-year truce with Byzantium, but was destroyed by a storm.

Exactly a hundred years after the initial assault the first Arab settlement on Sicily was established, at the port of Mazara on the south-west coast, and four years later the emirate of Sicily was founded with Mazara its capital. Mazara still has Arabic architecture and its central market is still called the *casbah*. (And it is again full of Muslim settlers crossing the western Mediterranean from north Africa.)

The emirate, despite its grandiose name, in reality only controlled the south-western corner of the island, but then another company of Arabs invaded Sicily yet again, and extended Arab control. This time, they had the excuse of an invitation. The former commander of the island's fleet, Euphemius, who had been dismissed after eloping with a nun, revolted in umbrage against the Byzantines and appealed for support from the Muslims in north Africa. The Muslim rulers saw this as a chance to expand and as a means of alleviating the criticisms of their military establishment and Islamic scholars who were united in clamouring for a campaign of *jihad*. So a fleet of a hundred Arab ships crossed to Sicily.

Though the invaders did not have things entirely their own way they were able to repel Byzantine counter-attacks, in one of which Euphemius was slain, and, with the aid of reinforcements from north Africa and Al-Andalus, they took Palermo, which became the capital of a new Muslim province. With many Arabs now settling on the island, Palermo developed into a major cultural and political centre of Islam, and before long Muslim forces based in Sicily had crossed to mainland Italy, over-run its southernmost regions and had even crossed from its western coast to the eastern and sailed the Adriatic to the southern Dalmatian coast.

Meanwhile, another huge Abbasid fleet had appeared in Byzantine waters and captured Crete, quickly spreading over that island as well, forcibly imposing Islam, killing any man who refused to convert and enslaving the women and children. Crete became full of Muslim pirates from whom no island or harbour in the eastern Mediterranean was safe. The Byzantine government sent a few expeditions to aid the locals but its navy could not cope with the strongholds of Crete and Sicily simultaneously and was unable to mount a sustained effort to drive back the Muslims, who over the next three decades raided Byzantine possessions almost unopposed.

In Sicily the contest between Christian and Saracen was to continue for another fifty years and is still fought nightly in the traditional puppet-shows of Palermo. The Muslims increased their pressure against the eastern parts of the island and, after a long siege, in 878 captured Syracuse. The last major Byzantine fortress, Taormina, fell in 902. Isolated fortresses remained in Byzantine hands until 965 but after the fall of Taormina the island was under Muslim rule and Sicilian culture became Arabicised. Christians in the north-eastern corner resisted Islamisation the longest, and the level of Arab influence varied across the island depending on the extent of Arab settlement and the length of resistance. Many Arab-derived names are in western areas, with a mixture in the south-east, while Christian identities survived strongest in the north-east, where the Byzantines retained control of some fortresses for a few decades and made several efforts to recover the island but were unable to seriously challenge Muslim control over Sicily. Christians from other parts of the island assembled in the north-east, which remained in contact with Byzantine southern Italy up until successive Arab invasions of the mainland led to the formation of the emirate of Bari.

And Arabs significantly impacted the genetics of Sicily and the south of the mainland. Apart from their sheer numbers, so many of them raped native women that their genes are still seen in the population. To this day northern Italians derisively call people from the south 'Saracens'. And the mafia practice of extorting protection money widespread in Sicily and Naples and on the Amalfi coast evolved from the original protection racket, the *jizya*. The word mafia comes from a new language that developed, Sicilian-Arabic. The Arabic word *ma'fi* means 'exempted'.

By then, the Abbasid caliphate, though remaining important religiously, was losing almost all its temporal political power, broken up into fragments ruled by rival autonomous dynasties through constant internal dynastic struggles, including an eight-year civil war between two brothers, and incessant conflicts between rival Muslim principalities.

During the civil war the eventual successor, a third brother named Abu al-Mutasim, the last strong Abbasid caliph, saw how his defeated older brother had been abandoned by his conventional army, including his bodyguards, when the tide turned against him. Al-Mutasim's solution to this problem was to recruit and train slaves as élite soldiers. These slave-soldiers were called *mamlukes*, an Arabic word meaning 'owned' or 'property' used as a recognised euphemism for slaves.

The Islamic prohibition on enslaving freeborn Muslims meant that for reasons of both religion and expediency, *mamlukes* had to be from outside the caliphate, either prisoners of war, captured in raiding expeditions or bought from slave traders, often Vikings, and many were acquired as boys from varied ethnic backgrounds ranging from north Africans on the coast of the Mediterranean to tribes from the Altai region of south Siberia. Enslaved boys came from Greece, Albania, Persia, Armenia, the Russian steppes, Sudan and Kazakhstan.

These youths were then taken to Abbasid towns such as Baghdad to start their indoctrination and training as fierce warriors. Immediately on arrival they were expected to learn Arabic and speak only that language, thus cutting one tie with their former lives. Few would ever see again their family or homeland.

Using these well-trained *mamlukes*, in 834 al-Mutasim suppressed an uprising in Mesopotamia and then, four years later, having evidence of their worth, he had many *mamlukes* in his army as he rode out of his palace at Samarra, deep in Mesopotamia upriver on the Tigris north of Baghdad, with the intention of reducing to rubble Amorium, the home of the family of Emperor Theophilus and the second city of the Byzantine empire, 200 miles south-east of Constantinople. Al-Tabari wrote that he had 'Amorium' painted on the shields and banners of his army, which was estimated at 50,000, with an equal number of camels and 20,000 mules.

The campaign began in late June, with a smaller force attacking through the Hadath pass in the east while the caliph with the main army crossed the Cilician Gates, a pass through the Taurus mountains connecting the low plains of Cilicia to the Anatolian plateau by way of the narrow gorge of the Gökoluk river. The two-pronged attack took Theophilos by surprise. He tried to confront the smaller force first but suffered a major defeat in torrential rain at the Battle of Dazimon on 22 July, barely escaping with his life when he saw that his opposite wing was in difficulties and led 2,000 men round to reinforce it without telling his junior commanders what he was doing. His unexpected disappearance gave rise to a rumour that he had been slain. Panic and flight inevitably ensued and when the rain ceased Theophilus saw that he and his men were surrounded. He was able to fight his way out because the Muslims' bowstrings were soaked and useless, but the battle was lost and al-Mutasim was already marching on Ankara en route to Amorium. A week later, Ankara, which had been left defenceless, surrendered and was plundered.

The Muslim army then besieged Amorium. The siege was fiercely contested, even after the Muslims, informed by a defector, effected a breach in a weak spot of the wall. After a fortnight, the Muslim troops successfully stormed the town. Many inhabitants sought refuge in a spacious church, in which they were burnt alive by the Muslims. Six thousand others were taken captive with the intention of selling them as slaves.

According to al-Tabari, al-Mutasim now considered extending his campaign to attack Constantinople but a conspiracy led by a nephew was uncovered and he abandoned his campaign, instead herding his captives on the long, arduous trek back to Samarra. The prisoners suffered during the march through the arid countryside of central Anatolia. Some became so exhausted they could walk no further and were slain. Others were slaughtered when the army's water supplies threatened to run low, or were left to die of thirst in the desert. Eventually, al-Mutasim was so annoyed by some captives escaping he massacred most of the rest, and only forty-two survived the journey back to Samarra. After seven years' captivity during which they steadfastly refused to renounce Christianity they were finally offered the choice of conversion to Islam or death. All without hesitation chose to die, and in March 845 were beheaded on the banks of the Tigris.

Theophilus took the fall of Amorium as a personal affront and, seriously alarmed, immediately sent an impassioned plea for assistance to the Western emperor, Lewis the Pious, proposing a joint offensive. The Byzantine envoys were received warmly at Lewis's court in June 839, and the talks continued spasmodically for another four years, despite both emperors dying in that time, but came to nothing. Al-Mutasim made no immediate attempt to follow up his victory until 842, when a huge fleet sailed against Constantinople from Syrian ports. A sudden storm smashed all but seven ships to pieces. Al-Mutasim never heard of this disaster, for he had died in Samarra after ordering the assault.

His son and successor, Mutawakkil, attacked Italy every year, in 846 sending a strong force to raid Rome's port, Ostia. The raiders struck as the Roman militia hastily retreated to the safety of the city walls. Some of Rome's treasures were outside the walls and easy targets. Another Arab raid against Ostia was repelled three years later.

Ten years after that a savage Muslim warrior named Abbas ibn Fadhl, who plundered lands and towns still under Byzantium's control, after several attempts and a long siege captured the fortress town of Castrogiovanni (now Enna) towering above the surrounding countryside in the centre of Sicily. The town was taken by Muslim troops who sneaked in through a sewer. All the adult male survivors were killed for resisting, and the women and children sold as slaves. Byzantium had tried to aid the stricken fellow Christians but its army was defeated.

By now Mutawakkil had unwisely promoted the bravest, boldest and most capable *mamlukes* to high ranks. History had already shown that creating élite units was fraught with danger. Rome's Praetorian Guard was soon making and deposing emperors and became the real power in Rome. Clearly, Mutawakkil was not a student of history. High-ranking *mamlukes*, especially those in the imperial bodyguard, were now in a position to turn on their masters and, in 861, Mutawakkil was murdered by his *mamluke* guards at Samarra while drinking with friends.

Other examples of *mamluke* treachery followed. Six months later they poisoned Mutawakkil's successor, Muntasir, following which the next caliph to be appointed, Mustain, fled to Baghdad to try and rally support. Meanwhile, the *mamlukes* chose and installed a caliph of their own, whom they felt would be more favourably disposed towards their interests. With this new leader, Mutaz, they besieged Baghdad, where Mustain was deposed and murdered. Mutaz soon proved to have his own ideas, one of which was to bring the army under control and restore the caliph's authority. In 869 the *mamlukes* murdered him as well. The next caliph, Muhtadi, also tried to assert his authority and the following year, he too was killed. With imperial guards murdering and making caliphs, soon there was anarchy in the caliphate, and it lost control of its western dominions, where the armies of megalomaniac Muslim leaders serially slaughtered each other in constant ferocious, bloody civil wars.

In Morocco Idris ibn Abdulla established an independent emirate, and his successors reigned for nearly two centuries, not acknowledging even the nominal sovereignty of the Baghdad caliphs. The Idrisids were twice forced to submit to another caliphate, the Fatimid, but each time regained control. The Idrisids finally succumbed to a native Berber tribe, former nomads of the Sahara who had settled on the coast and become Muslims, and it was the Fatimids who for 200 years were the dominant caliphate. North Africa, Egypt and much of Arabia were at one point presided over by the Fatimid dynasty, an empire stretching from Morocco to Yemen. The Fatimids also continued Muslim incursions into southern Europe, in 934 seizing and sacking Genoa. In Egypt, in 969, they established a new capital next to Fustat, calling their new city al-Kahira, 'the Vanquisher', supposedly because Mars, *an-Najm al-Kahir*, 'the Conquering Star', was rising at the time it was founded. The name later became anglicised to Cairo.

Though the Abbasids had kept their religious influence, their political power had weakened so much they were forced to cede authority in Egypt to the Fatimids, which was why the Fatimids could make their capital so near to Fustat, an important Abbasid town. Thanks to its close proximity to the Fatimid capital, for a century Fustat was a major production centre of Islamic art and ceramics, and one of the richest towns in the world. Recent archaeological digs have turned up Fustat trade artefacts as far away as Spain, China and Vietnam. Excavations at Fustat have also revealed intricate blueprints in which houses and streets were laid out in grids.

The Fatimids were of the Shi'ite denomination and understood themselves as legitimate caliphs, that is, as supreme leaders of global Islam. In this, they challenged the claims of the Abbasid caliphs of Baghdad, who were Sunnis who rejected Fatimid beliefs and practices.

The editors of the giant *Times' Atlas of World History*, which measures 15 inches x 11 inches, admitted the political divisions of the Muslim world in these centuries were too numerous to be shown on a single map even on their large pages, and listed the most important caliphates instead. There are thirty-eight of them. Throughout history Muslims have warred among themselves as well as constantly attacking infidels. During the tenth century Muslims rampaged around Europe, between 952 and 960 occupying Switzerland. In Europe the *jizya* tax was higher than anywhere else in the world.

And everywhere Muslims went they acquired slaves.

Slavery had been ubiquitous throughout the world since antiquity. In most cultures people did not enslave their own. Slaves were usually foreigners, and Muslims' slaves had to be non-Muslims. European Christians and African heathens were taken in the usual way, by conquest, Arabs enslaving so many Africans that one Arabic word, *abd*, came to mean both slave and negro. In the ninth century, high-ranking Abbasid bureaucrat and geographer Ibn Khordadbeh gave a precise account of trade routes. As Director of Posts and Police for an Abbasid province he was in a good position to know about them. And in his *Book of Roads and Provinces* he mentions casually in passing slaves as being among the merchandise: 'These merchants speak Arabic, Persian, Roman, Frankish, Spanish and Slav languages. They journey from west to east, from east to west, partly on land, partly by sea. They transport from the west eunuchs, female slaves, boys, brocades, castor, marten and other furs, and swords.' When the richest man in the world, Mali ruler Mansa Musa, as a good Muslim went on a pilgrimage to Mecca, he took with him 12,000 slaves. On his way back he could have bumped into Muslim traveller and writer Ibn Battuta, who, on returning home to Morocco from central Africa, on the last leg of the journey for safety joined a big caravan, which included 600 African female slaves. Battuta himself, as well as having many concubines and wives, also bought a 20-year-old Greek girl to use as a sex slave.

Russian slaves were supplied by the piratical Vikings, who realised there was a good market for living captives rather than corpses. They eased up on the slaughter and started taking prisoners instead and selling them to Muslims. Russians were initially pagans and, later, Christians. Either way, they were conveniently not Muslims and so fair game for enslavement. Russia became Christian when its ruler, Vladimir the First, in choosing a state religion, rejected Islam because of its prohibition of alcohol, declaring in a rhyming couplet:

Rusi yest vesole piti,
Bez nevo ne mozhet biti.

('Russians are happier drinking. They just cannot live without it.')

Apart from *mamlukes* and general slaves who would be domestic servants, labourers and so on, specific kinds of slave were in great demand by Muslims. These were adolescents, pretty if female and sturdy if male – and eunuchs.

Top officials and rich merchants kept *harems*. To defend these secluded groups of attractive bored women they needed men who were unable to seduce them. Castrated slaves had always served this purpose throughout the Middle East. Thomas Mann in his epic novel *Joseph and his Brothers*, set in ancient Egypt, describes one, a dwarf named Dudu who greets Joseph on his arrival as Joseph is himself about to be sold into slavery.

Muslims were unwilling to perform the operation themselves, for two reasons – religious and practical. Islam forbade it and the death rate among castrated adults was high, either from infection or post-operative complications such as the urethra becoming blocked and the slave's bladder bursting as a result. For adults, the mortality rate could be as high as 90 per cent. Even when the procedure was carried out skilfully by an experienced practitioner, most of those subjected to this hideous operation, performed without anaesthetics, did not survive. And a dead slave was a bad investment.

The solution to these little difficulties was to buy ready-made eunuchs from slave traders.

For three centuries the castration of slaves was big business. 'Castration houses' flourished in Venice and the French town of Verdun, producing eunuchs to sell to Muslims. These slaves were pre-pubescent, for the highest rate of success when creating a eunuch is when boys who have not yet begun puberty are used, when the shock to the system is less and the survival rate better. The prognosis depends also upon which methods are used and how extensive the operation is to be. In some of the earliest records of castration, the testicles are merely crushed and rendered useless. No loss of blood occurs and though it is agony the risk of death is minimal. The ancient Assyrians used this technique. Another procedure was to open the scrotum with a small incision and then scoring the testicles until they were so damaged they simply withered away. The mortality rate from such operations was low.

Unfortunately, these methods did not suffice for eunuchs required for service in Muslim *harems*. To claim that a eunuch's testicles were useless and damaged beyond repair was inadequate. Nor was it enough for the testicles to be removed. Before a eunuch could be employed, an inspection had to be carried out to confirm that not only were the testicles and scrotum completely absent but that the whole of the penis had also been amputated. Also, inspections were carried out periodically to ensure that the penis had not started to grow back. This ruthlessness about the extent of castration was because that even with no testicles a man can still sometimes have an erection so firm he can have intercourse. Radical castrations in which even the stump of the removed penis barely remained was the most effective way of ensuring that the *harem* ladies were not molested by those employed to guard them.

Short-term problems with the urinary tract could often be prevented by inserting a small plug in the urethra immediately after the penis had been amputated. This was kept in for three days and the boy not allowed to drink or wee in that time. When the plug was removed and urine flowed, the danger of death by a ruptured bladder had passed. From then on, and for the rest of his life, to have a wee the castrated boy would have to sit or squat like a female. Incontinence was common and for many the plug became permanent, only being removed in order to wee. Most suffered leakage at other times and eunuchs usually smelt of piss.

Many of the captives being bought and sold in the slave markets of north Africa were Spanish.

The myth of a tolerant, peaceful Muslim Spain, Al-Andalus, under nice, enlightened Muslim rulers bringing peace and prosperity to Spain does not match the reality. Even Maria Rosa Menocal, in her romantic and fantastical hagiography of Muslim Spain, *The Ornament of the World*, while arguing for the prevalence of *Convivencia*, a peaceful and beneficial coexistence, acknowledges the second-class status to which Christians and Jews were relegated. As well as paying the protection money, the *jizya* poll tax, Christians were prohibited from trying to convert Muslims, from building new places of worship, from displaying crosses (both on their persons and on their churches) and from ringing bells: 'In sum, they were forbidden most public displays of their religious rituals.'

The first Muslim conquerors of Spain, the Umayyad Arabs owing allegiance to distant Damascus and then the independent Umayyad state set up by al-Rahman, were followed by various waves of Moors, beginning with the Almoravids, a dynasty of Saharan Berbers who had emerged from a new puritanical Muslim movement and conquered the western Maghreb, north-west Africa, now Morocco, founding Marrakesh as its capital. In 1085 the Muslim leaders in central Spain sent them a plea to help repel the Christian armies of the *Reconquista* that were gradually moving south from northern Spain. Five years later the Almoravids took control of the whole of Al-Andalus, while keeping their capital at Marrakesh.

Their main adversary was a Castilian aristocrat named Rodrigo Díaz de Vivar, who in 1094 briefly reclaimed Valencia from their control. They called him *Al-Sayyid*, 'the lord', an epithet that Spaniards came to use too, pronouncing it El Cid, which is what he is known as in history.

Almoravid men veiled themselves below the eyes, a custom they adapted from southern Berbers. Although practical for the desert sand and dust, Almoravid men insisted on wearing the veil everywhere, as a way of emphasising their puritan credentials. It served as their uniform. Under their rule in southern Spain, sumptuary laws forbade local women from wearing the traditional lace veil, in order to make the Almoravid men's veil the distinctive dress of the conquerors. The Almoravids were defeated in 1147 by another Berber dynasty, with the confusingly similar name of Almohads, who also made Marrakesh their capital.

After the pope called Christian knights throughout Europe to a crusade in southern Spain, Sancho VII of Navarre and Peter II of Aragon, former rivals of King Alfonso VIII of Castile, joined Alfonso in a campaign against the Almohads that culminated in the 1212 Battle of Las Navas de Tolosa.

The Christian coalition crossed the mountains that defended the Almohad camp through a secret pass led by a local shepherd who knew the area and caught the Muslims by surprise at dawn. The tent of the caliph, al-Nasir, was surrounded by a bodyguard of *mamlukes*. Sancho's Navarrese force broke through this bodyguard. Al-Nasir got away but the Muslims, now leaderless and demoralised, were routed, suffering heavy losses. The victorious Christians sent to the pope al-Nasir's ornate tent, a sumptuous tapestry that it contained and a Muslim standard. They lost only about 2,000 men but their losses were particularly heavy among leading knights.

Al-Nasir died suddenly in Marrakesh the following year, having tried to play down the significance of the defeat, with assassination strongly suspected. He was aged only 32 and had no wounds or illness. The suspicion was heightened eleven years later when his son and successor also died young and suddenly and it was put about that he had been accidentally gored to death while playing with a pet cow.

The great Christian victory at Las Navas de Tolosa largely destroyed Almohad control over Islamic Spain. Though Muslim rump states survived in Spain for another 280 years, major Muslim power was broken.

The Nasrid dynasty, an Arab dynasty, was the last Muslim dynasty in Iberia, ruling the emirate of Granada from 1230 until 1492. Today, the most visible evidence of the Nasrid dynasty is part of the Alhambra palace and fortress complex built under their rule.

The name Alhambra derives from the Arabic *al-Hamra*, meaning 'The Red One', because of the reddish colour of its walls, which were built of rammed earth. The colour comes from the iron oxide in the local clay used for this type of construction.

The extravagant ornamentation of the courtyards of the Alhambra and the idyllic appearance of its gardens encourage visitors' reveries about a paradisal existence enjoyed by the Nasrid rulers but such reveries are founded on illusion. The rulers dwelt in a poisoned paradise, and most came to a violent end, called 'the Red Death' after their ruddy palace. The life expectancy of their viziers was not so good, either. In the fourteenth century Ibn al-Khatib, a vizier, mystic and poet who played an important role in the design of the most spectacular parts of the Alhambra, was hounded out of office by his assistant, a poet named Ibn Zamrak, whose verses appear in various parts of the Alhambra. Zamrak, who then assumed the office of vizier, had al-Khatib murdered in a Moroccan prison, but later Zamrak and his two sons were murdered in front of his wives and daughters. The political regime of Nasrid Granada is best characterised as a despotism tempered by assassination.

Three years after the warring kingdoms of Castile and Aragon were united by the marriage of Ferdinand the Second of Aragon with Queen Isabella of Castile, they joined forces in a campaign to remove this last remnant of Muslim Spain. When the bellicose ruler of the kingdom of Granada, Muley Abul Hassan, besieged a town twenty-five miles away from the city of Granada, the combined armies of Ferdinand and Isabella went to its assistance, forcing him to withdraw. Incessant warfare continued for a decade, Christian successes facilitated by protracted internal civil war between Hassan and two rivals for the Granada throne, his brother, Zagal, and his eventual successor, his son, Boabdil. To remove the Muslims the Spaniards created a highly efficient military force, and in overwhelming numbers they besieged Granada, repelling all desperate Muslim sorties. Boabdil's surrender of the city ended eight centuries of Muslim occupation of Spain, completing the long *Reconquista*. The spot from which he last saw Granada after handing over the keys still bears the name of *el último sospiro del Moro*, 'the last sigh of the Moor'. He died in battle in Africa two years later.

Free of the encumbrance of the Muslim yoke, Isabella sponsored Columbus's expedition to the New World, soon to be named after merchant and explorer Amerigo Vespucci, an Italian whom she made a citizen of Castile by royal decree and then appointed to the newly-created position of chief navigator for Spain's *Casa de Contratación*, House of Trade, in Seville.

After the regaining of Granada, Islam was outlawed in Spain. Muslims were expected to leave or become Christians. For a century those who remained, called Moriscos, though they outwardly became Christians not only continued to hold fast to Islam surreptitiously but plotted to take Spain back to Muslim rule. To pass as Christians a sustained performance by Moriscos was required, involving much subterfuge. After their babies were baptised as Christians they held a ceremony in which they removed its supposed effects by washing the baby and performing ritual ablutions, after which they would give the child a secret Muslim name. Dissimulating Moriscos included the privileged, the powerful and the learned, all pretending to be happy as part of a Christian society. The Moriscos' feigned adherence to Christianity allowed them to perform acts ordinarily forbidden or omit acts usually obligatory. Many Islamic legal stipulations were suspended. The Moriscos drank wine and ate pork, prayed with the Christians, uttered blasphemous Christian creeds, dispensed with the usual obligations connected with ritual and prayer if circumstances required, and even married their daughters to Christians.

For decades Moriscos were an incessant source of danger. While the Spaniards had always suspected that Islam prevented Muslims from being loyal to Christian rule, they also found out that many Muslims who had seemingly converted to Christianity were secretly plotting for the triumph of Islam, including by a military uprising with the aid of foreign Muslims, such as the neighbouring Berbers of north Africa, just across the Strait of Gibraltar. As a result, the Moriscos were expelled from Spain. Throughout these decades all Muslims knew that anyone among them who was quaffing rioja or scoffing chorizo was not doing it for enjoyment but was practising *takiya*, their hallowed licence to lie for Allah.

The final expulsions began in 1609. Three years earlier another classic example of deceit in the name of a deity had been exposed when the head of the Jesuit Order in England, Henry Garnet, was discovered telling lies to his examiners at his trial for treason, being a conspirator in Guy Fawkes' gunpowder plot. He alleged that he had done so in accordance with the doctrine of 'equivocation', which allowed Jesuits to say one thing while holding, but not uttering, mental reservations.

He continued to defend equivocation even in the week preceding his public execution, which was postponed for two days to 3 May to avoid a clash with another spectacle, the May Day celebrations. As he mounted the ladder to the scaffold he was urged not to equivocate with his last breath and he ruefully agreed that this was not the time to equivocate but that he had shown elsewhere how it was lawful and in what circumstances.

Father Garnet's dogged defence of equivocation was included in a publication known as the *King's Book*, an official account of the treason that thrust that specialised doctrine into the forefront of public consciousness. Powerful and essential reading, it told enough about the plot to convince Londoners and direct their thinking on the matter. One reader keen to take it up was William Shakespeare. The little quarto set him to thinking about equivocation, which, combined with the current immense interest in a Scottish king (James VI of Scotland, also newly James I of England), gave him a rare opportunity to write a play that chimed with the topical.

Throughout *Macbeth*, equivocation, the 'double sense' of Macbeth, the lying that Macduff's son refers to, is a principal mode of the operation of evil forces. *Macbeth* is a discovery or anatomy of evil. In *Macbeth* evil is all-pervasive. Of all Shakespeare's plays it is the one most obsessively concerned with evil. The whole kingdom lies under its interdict. No one knows what anyone else may mean, or what is true or false. *Macbeth* is filled with the idea of contradiction. Nothing is what it seems. In *Macbeth* Shakespeare makes clear that for evil to flourish on such a scale, 'double language', equivocation, must be widespread. The play actually begins with equivocation. In the opening exchange between the three witches they chant 'Fair is foul, and foul is fair'. And later in the play there is 'Lesser than Macbeth and greater' and 'These solicitings cannot be evil, cannot be good.'

Shakespeare showed in *Macbeth* that when equivocation is widely practised in a society, evil prevails.

And, as Islam permeates all aspects of Muslims' lives, equivocation, *takiya*, makes them stupendous liars. Though they eat no pork, they are forever telling porkies. No promise can bind them against the interest and duty of their religion, and they can abrogate their own contracts and agreements and those of their predecessors with an easy conscience. They regard endless deceit as service to Allah. To Muslims words are just another weapon of war. In all their dealings with the infidel, Muslims seek not the truth but the advantage. Outwitting or cheating an infidel is not considered reprehensible. Muslims come out with such brazen, outright nonsense that it seems inexplicable. They are programmed to be acutely sensitive to imagined slights and to retaliate out of all proportion, which is characteristic of paranoid schizophrenics. Whenever a Muslim seems to hold contradictory views simultaneously you never know if it is *takiya* or schizophrenia.

Backed by *takiya* Muslims will tell the most nonsensical, absurd, outrageous lies. A pretty *bint* named Irshad Manji said in an interview with journalist Bill Weir in an ABC News 20/20 documentary, *Islam: Questions and Answers*, that the famous notion that martyrs are pledged seventy-two virgins in paradise is based on a mistranslation, that in fact the pledge is for seventy-two raisins. As she said this, she gave the false smile that Muslims use, especially pretty females when lying to a male infidel. To achieve it, they draw their upper lip away from the teeth while looking at their interlocutor with charm. This Islamic smile turns them into an advertisement for toothpaste. The relevant passages in the *Koran* describe the delightful large breasts of these raisins. No wonder male Muslim martyrs consider getting to paradise their 'raisin d'être'.

Muslim leaders and Muslims in positions of power in Western countries brazenly contradict themselves, making one kind of speech to an audience of infidels and a hugely different kind to fellow Muslims.

Traditionally, *takiya* is used as a tactic when waging aggressive war and defensively by those feeling vulnerable, such as minority Shi'ites surrounded by a potentially hostile Sunni majority, and Muslims living in Christian lands.

Famous fourteenth-century Islamic scholar Ismail ibn Kathir wrote, 'Believers are allowed to show friendship to disbelievers outwardly, but never inwardly,' and quoted the seventh-century Abu Darda, who said, 'We smile in the face of some people although our hearts curse them' and al-Hasan al-Ashari, a prominent scholar and theologian who founded a school of tenets of faith that bears his name, who said, '*Takiya* is acceptable till the Day of Resurrection.' The *Koran* sanctions lying to infidels 'if it furthers the cause of Allah or the cause of that individual Muslim', adding, 'Allah has already ordained for you the dissolution of your oaths'. In Islam deceit is divinely mandated. This mandate makes a virtue out of immorality.

In the late sixteenth century, mysterious lead tablets were found in caves on a hill outside Granada with passages written in a curious version of Arabic and in parts unintelligible claiming to show that Arabs had lived in the town from as long ago as the time of Jesus. They purported to relate how St Caecilius was sent by St Peter as a missionary to Spain. Not only did the message of the tablets proclaim the Immaculate Conception of the Virgin Mary, but they also seemed to provide evidence that Arabs were the first Christians to arrive in Spain. They were forged by a prominent Morisco named Miguel de Luna.

Expulsions soon followed. Nowadays the expulsion of the Moriscos is portrayed as an act of Islamophobia, but the real reason was their plotting to restore Al-Andalus.

It had long been known throughout Europe that Islam was an inveterate enemy of Christianity. El Cid died on 10 July 1099 – five days before the first Crusade reconquered Jerusalem.

The Crusaders finally went on the offensive after 400 years of invasions and conquest, with carnage, massacres and atrocities and Christian armies fighting defensive battles that usually ended in defeat. All the lands that the Crusaders tried to recover were originally Christian lands that had been conquered over the course of the four centuries that preceded the first Crusade. As well as Iberia, the lands of Anatolia, Syria, Palestine, Egypt, Libya, Tunisia, Algeria and Morocco had been totally Christian. Now they were all totally Muslim. Christians were not the original aggressors. The Crusades were Christianity's response to invasions that began in the seventh century. By the time the first Crusade was launched in 1095 by the pope at the Synod of Clermont to spontaneous cries of 'God wills it!', which became the battle cry of the Crusaders, two-thirds of the known world was conquered, including many Christian lands.

The Crusades started 461 years after the first Christian city to be attacked, Damascus, was over-run by an Arab army, 457 years after Jerusalem was conquered by an Arab army, 453 years after Egypt was taken by Arab armies, 443 years after Arabs first plundered Italy, 427 years after an Arab army first besieged the Christian capital of Constantinople, 380 years after Spain was conquered by an Arab army, 363 years after France was first attacked by an Arab army, and 249 years after Rome was raided by an Arab army, which plundered the outskirts, prevented from entering the city itself by the Aurelian Wall.

Only after those four centuries of Arab armies burning churches and killing, enslaving, forcibly converting and raping Christians did the West respond with the Crusades. All the lands that the Crusaders tried to take back had been subjugated in the first place by Arabs.

Arabs, overblown with indignation, said they had ruled Jerusalem for more than 400 years as a justification for their right to it; but they had ruled it for more than 400 years because they had taken it from Christians all those years ago in conquest. The Crusaders *recovered* Jerusalem, which is named more than 800 times in the Bible and not once in the *Koran* (though it is alluded to as 'the further Temple' in the opening sentence of the chapter *Al-Isra*, (The Night Journey). And anyway it was not for long. After just eighty-eight years Saladin's Saracens recaptured it, due mainly to their *mamlukes*, who were expert horse archers and shock-action lancers, and the green banner of Islam again flew over Jerusalem. When the pope heard of the news of the fall of Jerusalem he died of shock.

During those 400 years the Arabs had not confined their depredations to Christian lands. Their armies inflicted great suffering on the East also.

A victory over a Tang Chinese army in a 751 battle at the river Talas at what is now the Kazakh-Kyrgyz border resulted in Muslim control of Transoxiana, the land beyond the river Oxus, now called the Amu Darya, economically beneficial because the region was on the Silk Road.

And Chinese prisoners of war introduced paper-making technology to the Middle East. Forty-four years later the first paper mill was built in Baghdad, a vital development for the circulation of the *Koran*. Unlike parchment and papyrus, the traditional materials used for the written word, paper was plentiful and easily produced. The *Koran* was now copied in great numbers and widely distributed. (In contrast, when the technology later reached Christian lands the ecclesiastical authorities there deemed paper inappropriate for bibles or liturgical volumes.)

Following the Muslim conquest of Central Asia, Sultan Mahmud of Ghazni became the first independent ruler of the Turkic dynasty of Ghaznavids, ruling from 998 to 1030. At the time of his death, his kingdom had been transformed into an extensive military empire.

From Ghazni, in present-day Afghanistan, he launched seventeen raids through the Punjab on what is now India, destroying, pillaging and massacring, zealously obeying the Koranic injunctions to kill idolators, whom he had vowed to chastise every year of his life. His biographer, Alberuni Yamini, proudly wrote, 'Mahmud utterly ruined the prosperity of the country and performed there wonderful exploits, by which Hindus became like atoms of the dust.' Yamini described some of these exploits:

At Thaneshwar 'the infidels' blood flowed so copiously that the river was discoloured, despite its purity, and people were unable to drink its water. The sultan returned with plunder that is impossible to count. Praise be to Allah for the honour He bestows on Islam and Muslims.'

At Mathura 'the infidels deserted the fort and tried to cross the foaming river but many were slain, taken or drowned. Nearly 50,000 men were killed.'

At Somnath 'the Muslims paid no regard to the booty till they had satiated themselves with the slaughter of the infidels and worshippers of the sun and of fire. The number of infidels killed exceeded 50,000.'

The extensive temple complex at Somnath contained a gilded statue of the Hindu 'great god' Shiva, served by 1,000 Brahmins, 350 entertainers and the revenue from 10,000 villages. Mahmud, after plundering his way through Gujarat, massacred Somnath's defenders and seized the temple. Precious stones and gems stored there were looted, the worshippers slaughtered, the gilded statue smashed to pieces (it is said by him personally) and the structure torched. The shards of the statue were then carried back to Ghazni, where they were incorporated into the steps of a new mosque. As well as slaying 50,000, the Muslims took back with them the same number of captives to be enslaved. After placing a new king on the throne in Gujarat as a tributary, to avoid enemy armies Mahmud led his force and captives on a detour through the Thar desert where many of the captives died of dehydration.

A full-scale invasion of India came at the end of the twelfth century that led to the formation of the Delhi sultanate.

The scale of the massacres in India cannot be imagined. They were so great that each took several frenzied days. Muslim historian Firishta (1560-1620) wrote that, between 1000 and 1500, 400 million Hindus were slaughtered. At the time of the first Muslim invasion India's population was 600 million. By the mid-1500s it was 200 million. Survivors were enslaved, the men castrated. 'The Islamic conquest of India is probably the bloodiest story in history,' wrote historian Will Durant. 'It is a discouraging tale, for its evident moral is that civilisation is a precious good, whose delicate complex order of freedom can at any moment be overthrown by barbarians, invading from without and multiplying from within.' And the foreign affairs editor of *Chronicles Magazine*, Serge Trifkovic, wrote too:

> These massacres perpetrated by Moslems in India are unparalleled in history. In their numbers, they are bigger than the Jewish Holocaust, the Soviet Terror, the Japanese massacres of the Chinese during WW2, Mao's devastation of the Chinese peasantry, the massacres of the Armenians by the Turks, or any of the other famous crimes against humanity of the 20th century. But sadly, they are almost unknown outside India.

Many of the Hindus who survived the massacres died while being marched north into slavery through deserts and the valley of the Hindu Kush, which means Hindu Slaughter. (None of this stopped historian William Dalrymple, writing on the BBC news website on 20 September

2015, calling the British 'the most powerful military force India had ever seen'.)

Meanwhile, another Muslim power menaced the West – the Seljuks, first mentioned as a nomadic tribe in the tenth century in Transoxiana. In the sixth century leadership of the nomadic Turkic tribes of Central Asia had been taken over by the Göktürks, who united them in the Göktürk empire. The Göktürk khanate was the first state known as 'Turk'. It eventually collapsed due to a series of dynastic conflicts but the name 'Turk' was later taken by many states and peoples, including the Seljuks, who originated from a branch of the Oghuz Turks on the periphery of the Muslim world, north of the Caspian and Aral seas in the steppes of Turkestan. When the Seljuk clan fell out with the Oghuz Turks, it split off from them and settled on the west bank of the lower Jaxartes (now Syr Darya), where, around 985, it adopted the prevailing religion, which was Islam. In the eleventh century, the Seljuks migrated to Persia where they encountered the Ghaznavid empire. They defeated the Ghaznavids in two battles, and after a successful siege of Isfahan established the Great Seljuk Empire. By 1045 they had spread across Persia; a decade later they were masters of Baghdad, establishing a protectorate over the moribund Abbasid caliphate. The Seljuks are ancestors of the present-day inhabitants of Turkey, which, though its people were called Turks for centuries, was not in fact named Turkey until 1923.

In 1064 Seljuk sultan Alp Arslan, whose flowing moustache was so long it had to be tied behind when he went hunting, led a huge expedition against Armenia and captured its capital, Ani, from where he advanced through Anatolia as far as the town of Caesarea in what is now north-central Israel that his forces sacked mercilessly.

New Byzantine emperor Romanus Diogenes fully recognised the gravity of the Seljuk menace but he had inherited a demoralised army, ill-fed, ill-equipped and often close to mutiny. Knowing that this army could never ensure the safety of Anatolia, he devoted his time to settling arrears of pay, producing new equipment and recruiting new forces. Meanwhile he laid plans for a campaign in which he would be able to send 70,000 men. In March 1071 that expedition headed eastward, where he split his army into two. The greater part he despatched under the command of one of his best generals, Joseph Tarchaniotes, to Khelat, a few miles from the northern shore of Lake Van, believing the Muslims might launch a counter-attack in that area, while he himself set off for the small fortress-town of Manzikert, which surrendered without a struggle.

No one knows what happened to Tarchaniotes' force. It vanished without trace. The men either deserted, fled or were beaten in an obscure battle. No information was sent to Romanus, only thirty miles away. All Romanus knew was that by the time he finally met the Seljuks he had lost more than half his army. The day after he had captured Manzikert his force suffered serious harassment from Seljuk mounted archers that continued through a moonless night. The Seljuks caused such tumult in the darkness that several times they were thought to have over-run the camp. In the morning it was a pleasant surprise to everyone to see that the palisades had held – but a disagreeable shock to learn that a big contingent of Turkic mercenaries had defected to the enemy; there were several other Turkic units in the army that at any moment might follow this example. In such circumstances one might have expected Romanus to welcome a Seljuk delegation that arrived a couple of days later proposing a truce. But he suspected typical Muslim trickery, and he was probably right. And anyway he wanted to settle the eastern question and the persistent Turkic incursions and settlements with a decisive military victory, and he understood that raising another army would be both difficult and expensive.

And so, on 26 August, he gathered his force into a proper battle formation and marched on the enemy positions, which were organised in a crescent formation. Muslim bowmen attacked the Byzantines as they drew closer; the centre of the crescent continually moved backwards while the wings moved to surround the Byzantine troops. By dusk the Byzantines had held off the arrow attacks and captured Alp Arslan's camp but the right and left wings, where the arrows did most of their damage, almost broke up when individual units tried to force the Seljuks into a pitched battle; the Seljuk cavalry simply disengaged when challenged, the classic hit-and-run tactics of steppe warriors. At dusk, with the Seljuks avoiding battle, Romanus was forced to order an organised retreat. But his right wing misunderstood the order and, thoroughly confused and suspecting betrayal by the army's untrustworthy Turkish auxiliaries, was almost immediately routed when the enemy seized the opportunity and attacked. The left wing held out a little longer but soon was also routed. The substantial rearguard, composed of 'levies of the nobility' led by a rival of Romanus, an ambitious young man named Andronicus Ducas, a nephew of the previous emperor involved in a conspiracy to usurp the throne, meanwhile deliberately ignored the order and marched back to the camp outside Manzikert rather than cover the emperor's withdrawal. Ducas had made no secret of his contempt for Romanus, and should not have been allowed even to join the campaign, let alone been given an important position.

Romanus stood his ground, calling in vain on his troops to rally. But the chaos and confusion were too great. A Byzantine soldier who survived described it:

> It was like an earthquake; the shouting, the sweat, the swift rushes of fear, the clouds of dust, and not least the hordes of Turks riding all around us. It was a tragic sight, beyond any mourning or lamenting. What indeed could be more pitiable than to see the entire imperial army in flight, the emperor defenceless, the whole Roman state overturned – and knowing that the empire itself was on the verge of collapse?

Romanus, left almost alone, refused to flee. Only when his horse was killed under him and a wound in his hand rendered him unable to hold his sword did he allow himself to be taken prisoner. His captors gave him no special treatment. All night he lay among the wounded and dying. In the morning, dressed as a common soldier and in chains, he was brought before the sultan, who at first refused to believe that the exhausted, bloodied and tattered captive covered in dirt who was flung at his feet was indeed the Roman emperor. Only when Romanus had been formally identified by former envoys and by a fellow prisoner did the sultan rise from his throne and, ordering Romanus to kiss the ground, place his boot on the emperor's neck. Romanus remained a captive of the sultan for a week, released only after the emperor promised that a vast ransom would be paid.

On his return home Romanus found his rule in serious trouble. Despite raising loyal troops, he was defeated in two battles against the Ducas family and was deposed, blinded and exiled to an island monastery 500 miles away where he soon died of an infection caused by his brutal blinding. Greek historian John Scylitzes wrote, 'Carried forth on a cheap beast of burden like a decaying corpse, his eyes gouged out and his face and head alive with worms, he lived on a few days in pain with a foul stench all about him.'

Pathetically, Romanus's last act was to gather all the money he could raise to send to Alp Arslan in proof of his good faith in paying his ransom.

The defeat at Manzikert was a disaster for the Byzantine empire. The consequences were stupendous. While rival claimants struggled for the Byzantine throne, the victorious Turks overran practically all of Anatolia, wiping out the heart of the empire. The Turks ravaged the country mercilessly, partly from barbarism, partly from policy. A great proportion of the population perished; the survivors fled.

Anatolia was depopulated; and the void was filled with swarms of Turkomen tribesmen – hundreds of thousands of them, all Muslim. Such tribesmen had been willing to serve in the Byzantine army as mercenary auxiliaries, albeit unreliable and untrustworthy, when they came from faraway Central Asia, but not when their homeland now bordered that of the Christian infidel enemy; and when parts of Anatolia were later regained, the Byzantines were unable to raise any significant forces from the region, which had been the principal native recruiting ground of the empire, where it had habitually raised armies of more than 120,000 men. From now on the empire was forced to rely almost exclusively on foreign mercenaries for the bulk of its armed forces – West Europeans for heavy cavalry, Pechenegs for light cavalry, Russians and Scandinavians for infantry. The most important permanent component of the imperial armies became the Varangian Guard, a name revealing the Norse-Russian origin of most of its members. The giant Harald

Hardradi, said to be seven feet tall, served in this guard from 1034 to 1042, commanding it in the last few years, three years later becoming sole king of Norway, having earlier shared the throne. In 1066 he invaded England, being slain at the exceedingly hard-fought and bloody Battle of Stamford Bridge in Yorkshire, a battle that depleted and exhausted the victorious English army, enabling it to be defeated in the Battle of Hastings on the south coast by the Normans just nineteen days later. Hardradi's only reward for his claim to the English throne was 'seven feet of English soil'. After the defeat at Hastings, many English soldiers joined the Varangian Guard, and in the later years of the Byzantine empire the guard was composed almost entirely of Englishmen.

The Seljuks were also constantly at war with Christian forces elsewhere in the world.

In the Holy Land, after a great victory by Prince Roger of Salerno at the Battle of Tell Danith in 1115, when his Crusader army surprised and routed a Seljuk army to preserve the Crusaders' hold on Antioch, the prince minted new coins bearing the image of St George and the dragon, the first Christian leader to depict this on his coinage, which infuriated the many Muslims in the region obliged to use it.

Four years later he perished in the Battle of Ager Sanguinis, the Battle of the Field of Blood, his army annihilated by the Muslim forces of Il-Ghazi, ruler of the Syrian town of Aleppo. The description Ager Sanguinis is a biblical reference to the field bought by Judas with the money he had been given to betray Jesus. The *Acts of the Apostles* records that Judas committed suicide in the field, and it is thus known in the Latin of the Vulgate as *ager sanguinis*. The Muslims' 20,000 troops heavily outnumbered the Christian army. They took 570 prisoners of war. As usual, knights were ransomed and the rank-and-file slain.

Il-Ghazi did not go on to defenceless Antioch, choosing instead to go on a drunken binge. Even so, because of the loss of the Antiochene field army, five towns rapidly fell into Muslim hands, which were recovered by Baldwin the Second after he narrowly defeated Il-Ghazi in battle six weeks later.

Despite this defeat and his reputation for drunkenness, Il-Ghazi was sent north to the Caucasus by the sultan to lead a Muslim coalition against the kingdom of Georgia. Unlike the neighbouring lands of Dagestan and Chechnya, which, ever since the Arab invasions of the seventh century had been populated by fierce Muslims, Georgia had, from the fourth century, remained staunchly Christian. The west of Georgia was the ancient land of Colchis, the home of the mythical Golden Fleece, derived from the local practice of using fleeces to sift gold dust from rivers, especially the Rioni, which flowed into the Black Sea.

For twenty years the Seljuks exacted an annual tribute from Georgia. King David the Fourth renounced this tribute in 1096/7, ended the seasonal migrations of the nomadic Seljuks into his kingdom, and in a series of campaigns from 1103 to 1118 secured several key fortresses. Then he launched a major military reform, resettling thousands of Kipchaks from the barren northern steppes to fertile frontier districts of Georgia, in return for which the Kipchaks provided one soldier per family, allowing David to establish a much-needed standing army.

The ceasing of paying tribute, banning of Muslim nomads and resurgence of Georgians' military energies provoked a Muslim response. In 1121 the sultan declared a *jihad* on Georgia. The Muslim coalition army under Il-Ghazi that was immediately formed and sent engaged the Georgian army in battle on 12 August in the narrow valley of Didgori, which in 1879 would become the birthplace, in a tiny shack, of the most famous Georgian, Iosif Dzhugashvili, who in adulthood was known first as Koba and then as Stalin.

At Didgori Il-Ghazi again saw the hated Christian image of St George and the dragon – on the Georgians' banners, for this was the kingdom's emblem. The battle, though hardly known elsewhere in the world, was one of the bloodiest in history, with casualties on the single day of fighting surpassing 200,000. Because of the narrowness of the valley, Il-Ghazi could not manoeuvre his cavalry, and, with David using effective tactics, Il-Ghazi's much bigger army was devastatingly defeated, and he himself wounded, the survivors mercilessly chased by Kipchak cavalry.

The victory at Didgori is celebrated in the *Georgian Chronicles* as a 'miraculous victory' and inaugurated the Georgian Golden Age, the apex of which was the long reign of Queen Tamar, who embarked on an energetic foreign policy aided by the decline of the Seljuks.

In 1149 Raymond of Antioch had allowed himself and his army to be surrounded by a Seljuk force, resulting in a massacre and his death, after which his skull, set in a silver case, was sent to the sultan in Baghdad as a gift; but in general Seljuk power was waning and twelve years later Sultan Kilij Arslan the Second was obliged to sign a humiliating treaty with Byzantium in which he returned all the Greek towns recently captured, forbade all further raiding and agreed to provide a regiment for the Byzantine army whenever required. To seal the agreement, he paid a state visit to Constantinople.

Emperor Manuel Comnenus resolved to impress him. He received his guest seated on a gold-plated throne set with sapphires and surrounded with pearls. A huge ruby hung on his chest. Twice a day during the three-month visit, the sultan's meals were served in vessels of gold and silver, all of which immediately became his to keep as a gift. The wonders of Greek fire were displayed at a water pageant. Circuses, tournaments and banquets provided further entertainment. A performance arranged by the guest was unfortunately less successful, when one of his entourage proposed to give a demonstration of flying. Swathed in a garment consisting entirely of pockets, in which the air was intended to support him, he climbed to a high platform and took off like Icarus. And, like Icarus, fell. When his broken body was carried away a moment later, it is said the spectators could not help laughing.

Chapter 3

Hulagu and Baybars; Othman founds the Ottoman empire; dhimmitude; Janibeg, the pioneer of biological warfare, infects Europe with the Black Death; Murad I and Bayezid I; the Siege of Rhodes; creation of the Janissary corps; the Battle of Kosovo; Tamerlane; Mehmed II and the fall of Constantinople

During the period of Seljuk decline another Muslim order, the Nizari, created an independent state, whose groups of activists, called *fidai*, became known for the judicious use of assassination. Marco Polo alludes to a drug used by the Assassins without naming it, and many readers and commentators have assumed that it was hashish and that the sect was named after it; but it is probably an etymological coincidence and the name is more likely to have derived from the Arabic word *asasiyyun*, meaning 'people who are faithful to the foundation [of the faith]'.

The Assassins' state was formed in 1090 after the capture of Alamut castle in modern Iran, a site that became its headquarters. Other castles became the foundation of a network of mountaintop fortresses throughout Persia and Syria that formed the backbone of Assassin power, notably including the Syrian stronghold at Masyaf near the Mediterranean coast. Rashid ad-Din Sinan is renowned as the greatest Assassin chief, though he could not keep Saladin off his territory.

While 'Assassins' typically refers to the entire sect, only the *fidai* actually engaged in murder. The sect lacked an army and relied on these hitmen to eliminate enemies. Stabbing by dagger was always the method of killing. Poison or arrows were never used, on principle.

Over the course of three centuries the *fidai* slew thousands of leading figures in the region, including three caliphs, a ruler of Jerusalem and many other Muslim and Christian chiefs. The first to be murdered in the effort to establish an Assassin state in Persia was Seljuk vizier Nizam al-Mulk in 1092. Raymond the Second, Count of Tripoli, was stabbed to death in 1152, and Conrad of Montferrat, *de facto* king of Jerusalem, forty years later. Saladin, a major enemy of the Assassins, escaped assassination twice, and Edward Plantagenet, the future king of England Edward the First, was also lucky to survive a *fidai* attempt to slay him.

In 1254 William of Rubruck, a Flemish priest on a mission to the Mongolian capital Karakorum, was struck by the security precautions in place there in response to a rumour that forty *fidai* had been sent to slay the Great Khan, Möngke, and two decades later Möngke ordered his brother, Hulagu, to lead a campaign to eliminate the Nizari state, which Hulagu duly achieved after great hardship and difficulties caused by the Nizari mountaintop strongholds, some of which were virtually impregnable.

Hulagu followed the destruction of the Nizari state with a campaign against the Abbasid caliphate.

By then many Mongols were Muslims. Contact with Islam began in the twelfth century when Muslim merchants took valued goods such as textiles and metal tools to Mongolia in exchange for furs. Conversions started in the 1240s. Contemporary Persian chronicler Juvaini wrote in his account of the Mongol empire, *History of the World Conqueror*, that in 1241 Khan Batu, while preparing for an assault on the Hungarians, climbed a hill to pray to the Mongols' supreme deity, Eternal Blue Heaven, and asked the Muslims in his army to pray for victory as well. By the end of the century, because of proximity, many Mongols in the west of the empire had converted to Islam. Most of the population in towns of the khanates were Muslims, ensuring that proselytisers had access to the Mongol leadership and to the military, including accompanying khans on campaigns and in their camps.

Berke, khan of the Golden Horde, was the first Mongol leader to officially establish Islam in a khanate of the Mongol empire, which caused a civil war with the new Ilkhanate founded and led by Hulagu after Hulagu sacked Baghdad, massacring more than 250,000 inhabitants and in a nearby village executing the last Abbasid caliph, al-Mustasim Billa. Berke sided with Muslim leaders rather than with brother Mongols (he was a cousin of Hulagu), signalling the end of the unified Mongol empire. If the Mongols had remained united they could have conquered the world, which Berke himself acknowledged.

Marco Polo wrote that Billa, a notorious miser, was immured with his treasures in an opulent tower to starve to death among his useless hoarded wealth, but it was more likely that he was tightly rolled in a carpet and either kicked to death or trampled to death by horses, as this was the usual method of the Mongols when killing a prince, in order not to shed royal blood, as Polo himself records in another passage.

Sir William Muir wrote in his 1896 *Mameluke Dynasty of Egypt* that Billa was 'a weak and miserly creature, in whose improvident hands the caliphate, even in quieter times, would have fared ill. We need not to travel beyond the imbecility of the caliph and the demoralisation of his now shrunken kingdom, for the causes of impending ruin.'

Billa combined an impolitic bluster towards the advancing horde with an utter failure to prepare the city's defences. He would have done better to confront the Mongols, who had noticed that Baghdad lacked the muscle to protect its accumulated wealth.

Hulagu was most unimpressed with his prisoner. A thirteenth-century intellectual, Nasir al-Din Tusi, recorded:

[Hulagu] set a golden tray of rotting food before the caliph and said, 'Eat!'

'It is not edible,' said the caliph.

Hulagu said, 'Then why did you keep it, and not give it to your soldiers before it went rotten? And why did you not make these iron doors into arrow-heads and come to the bank of the river so that I would not have been able to cross it?'

The caliph said, 'Such was Allah's will.'

And Hulagu replied, 'What will befall you is also Allah's will.'

Aleppo too was soon conquered, after the Mongols sent cats with burning tails running into the city to end the siege by fire. Damascus then quickly capitulated, after which Hulagu sought confrontation with the Mamlukes, the new rulers of Egypt and Syria.

The penultimate sultan of the Ayyubid dynasty, Malik al-Salih, in devoting himself to the reconquest of Syria had, like the Abbasid caliph Mutawakkil before him, unwisely promoted more and more *mamlukes* to high military ranks, making possible a successful coup, which happened when they assassinated his successor in 1250. The ensuing brief rule of al-Salih's widow Shajar ad Durr was the first time a woman had ruled Egypt since Cleopatra. But Billa and rebellious Ayyubid emirs demanded that she remarry and that her husband reign, and the principal *mamluke* regiments that had served al-Salih, the River Island and Tower regiments, forced her to marry their commander, Aybeg, who thereby became the first Mamluke sultan. His rule was disputed, the disputants supported by Shajar ad Durr, and on her orders he was murdered in his bath. She was then herself assassinated, beaten to death. More assassinations followed, until the vice-regent, Kutuz, brought the factions under his control, bloodily of course, with yet more political murders, to become the second Mamluke sultan.

High-ranking *mamluke*s had played a role in politics in the Islamic world since the ninth century but for the first time a system arose in which former slaves stood at the head of a self-perpetuating slave dynasty. This was unacceptable to Hulagu, and, from Syria, he sent envoys to Cairo demanding that Kutuz surrender. Kutuz slew the envoys, displayed their heads on a city gate, hastily mobilised and set out for Syria.

At this point, hard-riding messengers from the steppes of Central Asia fetched news that Great Khan Möngke had died, and Hulagu returned to Karakorum with some of his army to join in the inevitable dynastic struggle, won eventually by Möngke's younger brother Kublai. The remaining Ilkhanate army in Syria was still formidable, numbering about 25,000 men under Hulagu's lieutenant, Ket-Buka, west of the Euphrates.

The Mamluke and Ilkhanate forces met in battle at Ain Jalut, 'Spring of Goliath', in south-eastern Galilee in the Jezreel valley in September

1260. The battle lasted from dawn till midday. The Mamluke general, Baybars, feigned retreat (a favourite tactic of the Mongols, from whom he learned it) and led the Ilkhanate army into an ambush that was sprung from three sides, destroying it with a series of well-timed charges co-ordinated by an impressive command and control mechanism. Fire was used to trap Mongols who were either trying to hide or flee the field. Ket-Buka was captured and executed.

According to contemporary Syrian Arab chemist and engineer Hasan al-Rammah the Mamlukes used hand cannon at Ain Jalut, making it the earliest known use by Muslims of the first true firearm, though in this case the guns were fired merely to frighten the Mongol horses with the noise. They had no trigger, requiring direct manual external ignition through a touch hole. Al-Rammah also gave the composition of the gunpowder, instructions for the purification of saltpetre and descriptions of gunpowder incendiaries. His use of terms suggests he got his knowledge from Chinese sources. He calls saltpetre 'Chinese snow', fireworks 'Chinese flowers' and rockets 'Chinese arrows'. In his *Book of Military Horsemanship and Ingenious War Devices* he includes twenty-two gunpowder compositions, the median of seventeen of which is nearly identical to the modern reported ideal gunpowder composition of 75 per cent potassium nitrate, 10 per cent sulphur and 15 per cent charcoal. Ironically, it was invading Mongols who introduced gunpowder to the Islamic world. It had been used in China as early as the tenth century, initially only for demolition and the bang in fireworks. The first gunpowder weapon was a long-barrelled bamboo musket invented by a general commanding a besieged garrison in 1132.

As the victorious Mamlukes returned to Cairo, Baybars murdered Kutuz and seized the sultanate. This set the pattern of succession in the Mamluke empire. Only a few Mamluke sultans died of natural causes and one of those died from pneumonia brought on by permanently wearing armour to ward off assassination attempts. The average reign of the Mamluke sultans was a mere seven years. Mamlukes were not supposed to be able to inherit wealth or power but attempts to create lineage did occur and every succession was announced by internecine struggles. Purges of higher lords and rivals were common and anyone suspected of intrigue was crucified or impaled.

The Ilkhanate army at Ain Jalut was relatively small but the Mamluke victory had great psychological significance, for until then Mongols had been considered invincible.

As well as holding the Mongols at bay, Baybars destroyed the Christian lands of Outremer. In 1263 he captured Nazareth and destroyed the environs of Acre. In 1265 he captured Caesarea and Haifa. He then took the fortified town of Arsuf from the Knights Hospitaller and occupied the Christian town of Athlit. Safed was taken from the Knights Templar in 1266. He slaughtered Christians if they resisted and particularly hated the military orders, the Templars and Hospitallers receiving no quarter. His general, Kalawun, led an army into Armenia, capturing its capital in September. With the conquest of Armenia the Crusader city of Antioch was isolated. Baybars besieged it and it was taken after four days. All the inhabitants who were not killed were enslaved.

Acre was attacked again but withstood the assault. Jaffa fell in March 1268 and Beaufort the following month. In 1271 Baybars took the White Castle and Krak des Chevaliers from the Templars and Hospitallers after a month-long siege, and added to its already awesome fortifications. The Christians had shown that such powerful fortresses could break up insurgencies, make up for a paucity of forces and threaten enemy communication lines, and he followed the same policy with great success. All the north African Muslim states were also tributary to him.

Baybars was born in a Turkish tribe living in what is now Ukraine. Menaced by the Mongols, his tribe moved west and settled in Bulgaria. When he was 25 the Bulgarians fell out with his tribe, attacked it and sold many into slavery, including him. He was transported in chains to the Aleppo slave market, where he was sold to an Egyptian soldier and ended up in Cairo as a *mamluke*. When he seized the sultanate he was still only in his early 30s. He died after drinking by mistake a cup of poisoned wine intended for a guest.

His successor repelled an Ilkhanate invasion of Syria by a narrow victory at the 1281 Battle of Homs and continued the recovery of

Crusader territory, and the successor's son completed the eviction of the Crusaders from the Levant.

Meanwhile, more Muslim Turkomen tribes from Central Asia, fleeing before the Ilkhanate advance, had settled in the areas of no man's land in Anatolia, from where they made regular incursions into imperial territory for booty. Soon they justified these plundering raids as a form of *jihad*, regarding themselves as honourable 'warriors of the [Muslim] faith', *ghazis*. By the start of the fourteenth century all Anatolia had been engulfed in the *ghazi* tide, only a few major Byzantine strongholds and isolated Black Sea ports still holding out.

For Byzantium 1302 was a particularly bad year. In the early spring emperor Michael the Ninth launched a campaign that reached south to Magnesia. The Turks, awed by the size of his army, avoided battle. Michael sought to confront them but was dissuaded by his generals. The Turks, encouraged, resumed their raids, isolating him at Magnesia. His army dissolved without battle, the local troops leaving to defend their homes, and the recently hired Alan mercenaries to rejoin their families in Thrace. Michael was forced to withdraw by ship, followed by another wave of refugees.

And then, on 27 July, on a plain just outside the eastern Bosporus port of Nicomedia called Bapheus, a small Byzantine force encountered a Turkish army of 5,000 light cavalry, more than twice its size, commanded by a local *ghazi* emir named Othman, who had succeeded in the leadership of his clan in 1282 and over the next two decades launched a series of ever-deeper raids into the Byzantine borderlands of Bithynia to the north of Anatolia. By 1302 his clan was besieging the former imperial capital of Nicaea, north-east of Nicomedia and, by roaming the countryside, preventing the collection of the harvest, threatening Nicomedia with famine. It was to relieve the port that the Byzantines had sent the small force. The ensuing battle ended in a crucial defeat heralding the final capture of Bithynia by the Turks and clearing Othman's way south-west. He and his men surged along the Sea of Marmara until they reached the Aegean and the northern islands of Greece. Othman, having started out as ruler of one of the smallest *ghazi* emirates of Anatolia, had begun the campaigns that would give his name to the mighty Ottoman empire.

Hulagu and Baybars; Othman founds the Ottoman empire   69

Othman's father, Ertugrul, was a warlord from what is now Turkmenistan in Central Asia who conquered the Anatolian village of Sogut and its surrounding area. Sogut, where Ertugrul later died and has a resplendent mausoleum, grew into a city and under Othman became the Ottoman capital. A statue of Ertugrul is one of several of Turkmen heroes that surround the Independence Monument in the Turkmenistan capital, Ashgabat, and he is the hero of an immensely popular Turkish television film serial.

In 1343 a Muslim force, troops of the Mongolian principality the Golden Horde, besieged the Crimean port of Caffa, which was run by Genoese traders. The Golden Horde had captured Crimea in the 1230s, after which they allowed Genoese merchants to establish a trading settlement in Caffa (now Feodosiya), which became a major port monopolising trade in the Black Sea region.

In the region, as in all lands conquered by Muslims, locals who did not become Muslim were subject to a second-class status called dhimmitude. As well as all men paying the *jizya* tax, *dhimmis* had to obey humiliating regulations specifically designed to subdue them, including having doorways to their home built so low the *dhimmis* had to bend every time they entered or left to remind them of their lowly status, and when approaching a Muslim on a pavement it was always the *dhimmi* who had to give way.

Jews and Christians were given identifiable clothing. Yellow stars were first given to Jews in the ninth century in Iraq. The *jizya* tax was paid in a monthly ceremony where the *dhimmis* would humbly kneel and hand their money or goods to a *mullah*, who, if he was in a bad mood, might add a slap in the face to the ceremony as a reminder of who was in charge. In many areas Jews and Christians were given necklaces to wear as receipt that they had paid their *jizya* tax.

Any business transaction between a *dhimmi* and a Muslim always had to be to the Muslim's advantage, to the point that the *dhimmi*'s self-esteem actually suffered when trading with them, which was the Muslims' prime intention. In negotiations on business contracts, Christians spoke with Muslims only in the finest circumlocutions, calling the Muslim 'my lord' and speaking of themselves in the most disparaging terms. They sensed the Muslim liked this and it might make him more amenable to fair and equal terms. During the negotiating, Muslims avoided eye contact, glancing here and there but not into the Christian's face, so that afterwards no one knew whether the matters addressed were binding for either, since agreements made only with the lips and not with the eyes as well could not be considered valid and settled. Dealing with Muslims was painful. It seemed that, whatever the Christian said or did, the Muslim would always despise him. He could not win. In Muslim tradition, deceiving Christians was not sinful but permissible. An ancient document called Declaration of Immunity absolved Muslims from observance of all agreements made with Christians. Muslims were arrogant and preachy, who believed they had spiritual precedence over the rest of humanity. They never integrated. They were not harmless and tractable and were always disliked.

This would have been the atmosphere – resentment rife, conflict common – when, after decades of economic and religious tension between local Muslims, few of whom were Mongols, and Christian Genoese, a brawl took place in a trading station at the mouth of the Don named Tana, famous as the starting point of the land route to China. A fourteenth-century travel guide for eastbound merchants opens with, 'The road you take from Tana…'. According to an Italian notary, Gabriel de Mussis, a Muslim was fatally stabbed, and new Mongol Great Khan Janibeg, a self-proclaimed defender of Islam who had seized the throne the previous year by personally strangling his predecessor, who happened to be his brother, besieged Tana with a big force with an ultimatum that the murderer be handed over to him. An insolent response was sent back. The Mongols attacked, and the outnumbered Genoese retreated by sea westwards to Caffa, where they were granted protection. This was in itself a direct challenge to Islamic authority. Granting protection in a *dhimmi* land was the sole prerogative of the ruling Muslims. Protection was an integral part of the *dhimmi* system. The word *dhimma* originally meant 'compact' and is used twice in the *Koran* in this sense but its meaning broadened out to that of a compact giving a guarantee of security and by extension 'protection'. Once, in the seventh century, when the Arab invaders had to retire from the Syrian town of Homs they refunded the protection money that had been paid.

Janibeg, having pursued the fleeing Genoese overland, besieged Caffa and demanded that it hand over the culprits. Caffa refused. With access to the sea, Caffa was able to fetch in supplies and reinforcements from Italy, and Janibeg gave up. He returned with his army to the steppes.

Two years later he returned, to resume the blockade. This time, some of his troops were infected with the plague *Yersinia pestis*, which originated in the steppes, where it was endemic in rodents, spreading to humans in flea bites.

De Mussis wrote that after the plague broke out in the army Janibeg ordered infected corpses to be placed in catapults designed to throw boulders and fireballs over the walls of fortified cities, and lobbed into the crowded town. The defenders quickly dumped most of these bodies in the sea but the damage was done. Soon rotting corpses tainted the air, poisoned the water supply – and spread the disease. The stench was overwhelming. As the death toll mounted, bodies were stacked like firewood in public squares; feral animals ate human remains in the streets; old women dragged corpses of relatives through the rubble of the town shattered by the Muslims' bombardment; burning buildings spewed jets of flame and smoke into the sky; swarms of rodents staggered around with a strange bloody froth at their snouts…

This tactic of Janibeg was the earliest instance of biological warfare.

As the disease took hold in Caffa Genoese traders and seamen fled, sailing across the Black Sea and unknowingly taking the plague with them, introducing it first into Constantinople and then Europe. Galleys from Caffa reached Genoa, Venice and Pisa and at the end of January 1348 a galley expelled from Italy arrived in Marseilles, where the word quarantine was coined from the Latin *quadraginta*, forty, as forty days was the statutory length of time to remain isolated.

From France, the plague spread to Iberia. And that summer the *Chronicle of the Grey Friars at Lynn* recorded its arrival in England. The chronicle described how sailors from Gascony had disembarked in the port of Weymouth, Dorset, bringing with them 'the seeds of the terrible pestilence'. From the south coast the plague spread rapidly throughout England. Medieval chronicler Henry Knighton remarked how 'few lay sick for more than two or three days' before dying. According to another medieval chronicler, Thomas Walsingham, there were barely enough living to bury the dead.

Within two years the plague, later named the Black Death, halved the populations of the compatriots of Boccaccio and Chaucer. Boccaccio completed *The Decameron* in 1358. It consists of stories told to each other out of boredom over ten days by a group of seven women and three men isolating themselves at the Dominican Monastery of Santa Maria de Novella near Florence during the plague a decade earlier. Historian Ole J. Benedictow informs readers of his 2021 book *The Complete History of the Black Death* that only forty-four of the monastery's previous 130 inhabitants survived, a mortality rate of sixty-six per cent.

Chaucer, who began writing *The Canterbury Tales* in 1386, borrowed largely from *The Decameron*. In *The Canterbury Tales* twenty-four stories are told by pilgrims on their tedious horseback journey from Southwark in London to the shrine of martyr Thomas Becket.

About the time Chaucer was starting to write *The Canterbury Tales* the Genoese in Caffa took revenge for the initial deliberate spreading of the plague. They murdered former Golden Horde warlord Mamai after he had fled there following his defeat in a battle for leadership of the horde fought near the mouth of the Dnieper river at the Black Sea. (In twenty-one years of political turmoil within the horde, twenty-five khans succeeded each other.)

Yersinia pestis also depopulated Anatolia. And the 1302 defeat of the Byzantines by the Ottomans at Bapheus had led as well to an exodus of the Christian population from the area into the European parts of Byzantium, further altering the region's demographic balance. As the Byzantines lost control of the countryside of Bithynia they withdrew to their forts, which, isolated, fell one by one. The loss of the region allowed the Ottomans to achieve the characteristics and qualities of a Turkic Muslim state.

All Muslim states always shared one characteristic: whenever they felt strong enough they invaded other lands. It seemed as though they considered this a sacred duty. The Ottomans believed they had a divine mission to conquer the whole of Europe, and, under the flags of Islam, embarked on this mission. They quickly occupied much of the Balkans to lay the foundations of their empire, immediately acquiring a reputation for merciless ferocity. As early as 1354, Gregory Palamus of Thessalonica wrote,

> For these impious people, hated by God and infamous, boast of having got the better of the Romans by their love of God... they live by the bow, the sword and debauchery, finding pleasure in taking slaves, devoting themselves to murder, pillage, spoil... and not only do they commit these crimes, but even – what an aberration – they believe that God approves of them. This is what I think of them, now that I know precisely about their way of life.

In that year, under Othman's successor, Orhan, the Ottomans established at Gallipoli in the southern part of east Thrace their first permanent European settlement. Military campaigns had provided them with an intimate knowledge of the area, and they seized Gallipoli as a permanent foothold in Europe after Thrace had been devastated by a violent earthquake. Hundreds of towns and villages were destroyed. Few houses in Gallipoli remained standing. The disaster was made still more catastrophic by the conduct of the Turks. Orhan's son Suleiman Pasha immediately set off for the stricken lands, taking with him as many Turkish families as he could find. Most headed for the ruins of Gallipoli itself and, within a few months, the restored city had an exclusively Turkish population where a Greek one had been before.

For Byzantium this first Turkish settlement on the European continent was a greater calamity than the earthquake itself. To a demand for its restitution, Suleiman replied that he had not taken it by force, it had fallen to him through the will of Allah and to return it would be an act of impious ingratitude; his people had simply occupied a place abandoned by its former inhabitants. (Suleiman died in a hunting accident three years later.)

Gallipoli gave the Ottomans a strong bridgehead into mainland Europe, and they expanded rapidly in Thrace as the Byzantine empire became virtually an Ottoman fief.

In 1362 a new emir named Murad came to power. Styling himself Sultan, he soon proved to be energetic and determined, creating the Janissary corps, élite infantry units consisting of Christian boys taken from rural areas of the Balkans and brought up as Muslims, and the *devshirm* levy system through which they were conscripted. They were known as the *yeniseri*, the 'new corps'. Janissary is an English corruption of *yeniseri*. Initially, janissaries were expert archers, but they soon became the first troops to use guns extensively. In hand-to-hand fighting they used axes and a short scimitar called a *yatagan*.

Accounts of several battles of the period describe the janissaries as an impassable wall, protected by a trench and an earth embankment behind it, strengthened with iron stakes and big shields. The Ottomans placed their camels laden with rich baggage and sacks of gold behind the janissaries. Should the enemy reach the embankment, these were to be used to distract the enemy to buy time. The janissaries played an equally important role in siege warfare. Ordered to scale the walls of enemy fortresses during attacks, they regularly broke the resistance of defenders, leading to the capture of the fortress. And Murad's bodyguard was composed entirely of janissaries, 2,000 of whom accompanied him on his campaigns in the Balkans during the 1380s that culminated in the horrific 1389 Battle of Kosovo Field, 'the field of blackbirds'. A contemporary wrote, 'There were wars and battles but nothing like this.' The defending Serbs knew they could not win. They fought bravely, however, and most men on both sides died, the heavy losses more disastrous for the less numerous Serbs.

In Ljubomir Simović's epic novel *The Battle of Kosovo* a Serbian doctor making his way to the site of the impending battle is asked by guards why he was going there, and he replies:

> Do you know how many punctured livers, lungs, scattered guts and brains, broken hands and feet, broken ribs, crushed skulls, broken fingers and spines, dug out eyes and broken bones, shot through

throats and jaws there will be in Kosovo? There will be enough blood to sail on it with boats.

It was the Serbs' last stand. A Turkish victory over them in a battle by the Maritsa river in 1371 had utterly destroyed their army, the only barrier to the Muslims over-running Serbia, Macedonia and Greece. After it, the Serbian aristocrats, like those of the Byzantine emperor and the Bulgarian tsar, were vassals, obliged to pay tribute to the sultan and to lend him military assistance on demand.

It seemed impossible after the disaster at the Maritsa river that the Serbs would ever fight again but in 1389 a league of Serbian aristocrats put aside their many deep differences to gather under the leadership of Prince Lazar and marched to meet the Muslim army on the plain of Kosovo, where, in June, they were, inevitably, utterly defeated, perishing sacrificially, including Lazar.

For the few survivors, the only small consolation was that Murad did not live to enjoy his victory. One of the aristocrats, Miloš Obilić, sought an audience pretending he wished to defect and, before the Janissary guards could prevent him, on a day of extraordinary suicidal Serb courage, knowing he could not escape and would be decapitated, stabbed Murad in the stomach with a hidden dagger.

In Simović's novel the mortally wounded sultan says to his son, Bayezid, 'Behind Kosovo there are churches standing one behind another. Behind these Serbian churches are German, Roman, Florentine and Venetian churches. And churches in Paris and Rouen. Till when you hear no church bells, till then you will have to unleash the arrow of Islam.'

He then died, gazing forlornly down at his innards, which were slithering in his hands.

Bayezid, who was in charge of the left wing of the Muslim army, called his younger brother, Yakub, who led the other wing, to the command centre tent and there, in order to become the undisputed heir to the Ottoman throne, ordered an aghast janissary to strangle him.

Because Murad's intestines had slithered out of the hole in his belly they were buried in a corner of the battlefield while the rest of him was taken to the Ottoman capital for burial, so he has two tombs.

The news of his death was greeted with joy in Christendom: in Paris, King Charles the Sixth went so far as to order a thanksgiving service in the cathedral of Notre Dame. But tragic truths soon became known: that the Serbian nation no longer existed; that Byzantium was so reduced and demoralised as to be scarcely recognisable as the glorious empire it had once been; and that, given this weakness and the disunity of the West, Ottoman armies were by now invincible.

Bayezid obeyed his father's last wish that he 'unleash the arrow of Islam' on Christian Europe, including unsuccessfully besieging Constantinople for eight years. Impetuous in battle and unpredictable, he was called *Yildirim*, 'Lightning' or 'Thunderbolt'.

In the winter of 1393-94 he conceived an audacious plan – a massassination. He summoned his main Christian vassals, including Byzantine Emperor Manuel the Second and several of Manuel's relatives, to the Muslim camp at Serres in Macedonia. None knew that the others had also been summoned: only when they were all assembled did they realise they had put themselves completely in Bayezid's power. Manuel himself shared the general view that a massassination had been planned. Bayezid countermanded his own orders at the last minute. After giving his top vassals grim warnings of the consequences of disobedience, he let them go, and they returned home, shaken by their narrow escape from an ignominious death.

Recurring Ottoman raids had exposed the weakness of the Hungarian kingdom's borders, and King Sigismund set about strengthening them. Recent research has shown that whereas before 1390 there were only four castles between Severin and Belgrade, by 1429 fourteen castles guarded this section of the border. No other monarch had expended as much effort to ward off the Muslims. Himself aware of the importance of his struggle, his role as 'shield and rampart' and 'strong arm' of Christianity was recognised in 1410 by the pope.

The new defence line that the king established required a permanent military force in the border castles, which entailed hitherto unknown financial burdens for the treasury. A 1429 calculation estimated the costs of maintaining the border garrisons amounted to a third of Sigismund's ordinary revenues. To finance the border defence, he collected extra taxes nine times during his reign.

Also, from 1397 he took half of the ecclesiastical revenues to finance the wars with the Muslims and left archbishoprics and bishoprics vacant for years, allowing his frontier commanders to use revenues from these estates to pay their garrisons.

Alarmed at the Muslim expansion, Sigismund appealed to the princes of Christendom to form and join another late crusade. They responded positively, as did both popes. Though the Western Schism had split the papacy in two, with rival popes at Avignon and Rome and the time long past when a pope had the authority to call a crusade, the Roman pope proclaimed a new crusade, and, after two years of negotiation and preparation, a Christian army marched into the Balkans, with John, Count of Nevers, called John the Fearless, aged only 24, in nominal command. It consisted of Sigismund's 60,000 Hungarians, 10,000 French knights, 6,000 knights from Germany, and 10,000 Wallachians, with another 15,000 volunteers coming from England, Spain, Italy, Poland and Bohemia.

It halted its march in front of a Turkish-held Danubian fortress named Nicopolis, intending to capture it after a siege. Nicopolis, located in a natural defensive position, was a key stronghold controlling the lower Danube and lines of communication to the interior. The fortress was actually two walled towns, the bigger one on the heights of a cliff and the smaller below. The Turkish governor of Nicopolis was confident that Bayezid would come to its aid and was ready to endure a long siege. It was well-defended and adequately-supplied.

The Crusaders had brought no siege machines with them, and this lack, the steep slope up to the walls and the formidable fortifications made taking the castle by force impossible. They set up positions around the town to block the exits, and, with also a naval blockade of the river, settled in for a siege to starve out the defenders. Nevertheless, they were convinced that the siege of the fortress would be a mere prelude to a major thrust into relieving Constantinople and did not believe that Bayezid would arrive so speedily to give them a real battle. A fortnight passed as the bored Crusaders entertained themselves with feasts, games and shouting insults at the enemy. Through drunken carelessness they posted no sentries, though foragers and horsemen carrying out reconnaissance brought word of the Muslims' approach.

At a war council Mircea of Wallachia, a region of Romania, suggested a battle plan in which his infantry, who had experience in fighting the Muslims, would be sent in the first attack to meet the Muslim vanguard, which was usually a poorly-armed conscript militia called *bashi-bazouks*, normally used for pillage but deployed in battle to tire opponents before they met better-quality Muslim forces, including the élite janissaries. Sigismund supported this sensible plan, agreeing that this vanguard was not worthy of the attention of knights. But a haughty French aristocrat, Philip of Artois, Count of Eu, denounced the proposal as demeaning to the knights, who would be forced to follow peasant footmen into battle. Saying 'To take up the rear is to dishonour us, and expose us to the contempt of all', he declared that he would claim front place in the attack and anyone in front of him would do him mortal insult. Most of the other knights, including the greatest French soldier of the time, Jean le Maingre, thought likewise.

Their arduous charge up a steep slope crushed the *bashi-bazouks* in the Muslim front line and advanced into the lines of trained infantry, though the knights came under heavy fire from archers and were hampered by rows of sharpened stakes designed to skewer the stomachs of their horses. Chroniclers write of horses impaled on stakes, riders dismounting, stakes being pulled up to allow horses through, and the eventual rout of the Muslim infantry, who fled behind the relative safety of their heavy cavalry. Experienced French knights recommended that they pause to re-establish their ranks, give themselves some rest and allow the Hungarians time to advance to a position where they could provide support. They were overruled by the younger knights who, having no idea of the size of the Muslim force, believed that they had just defeated Bayezid's entire army and insisted on pursuit. The French knights thus continued up the hill, though accounts state that more than half were on foot by this point, either because they had been unhorsed by the lines of sharpened stakes or had dismounted to pull up stakes.

Struggling in their heavy armour, they reached the plateau at the top, where they had expected to see fleeing Muslim forces. Instead they found themselves facing a fresh corps of heavy cavalry, which Bayezid had kept in reserve. As this cavalry surged forward in a counter-attack to the sound of trumpets and kettle drums and yelling *'Allahu akbar!'* the desperation of the situation was apparent to the French and some knights broke and fled back down the slope. The rest fought on, 'no frothing boar nor enraged wolf more fiercely' in the words of one contemporary chronicler. Admiral de Vienne, to whom was granted the honour as the eldest knight of carrying the French standard into battle, was wounded many times as he attempted to rally the morale of his countrymen, before being struck down. Other notable knights were also slain. The Muslims threatened to overwhelm the young Count Nevers, and his bodyguard threw themselves to the ground in silent submission to plead for the life of their liege lord. The Muslims, aware of the riches that could be gained by ransoming captive aristocrats, took Nevers prisoner. Seeing him taken, the rest of the French yielded. Le Maingre was also captured, and both he and Nevers were duly ransomed. Philip of Artois, also taken as a prisoner of war, for some reason was not ransomed and subsequently died in a Muslim jail.

The Muslims executed the other Christian survivors, 10,000 in all, whom they first stripped naked. The victims were undressed slowly and carefully before being slain so that their clothes did not get bloody and could be worn by their murderers and any valuables in the pockets were not damaged. The killing, watched by Bayezid with short breaks for meals, went on from early morning until late afternoon, mainly by decapitation but also by hacking off a limb so that the victim slowly bled to death in agony.

Two years later the pope issued two bulls, again calling on Western countries to either take part in yet another crusade or, failing that, to send financial contributions for the defence of Constantinople. Charles the Sixth of France sent 12,000 gold francs with military aid, and le Maingre, longing for revenge for the humiliation of being made a prisoner of war, was sent with six ships carrying 1,200 men to try to help relieve the beleaguered city. He saw immediately on arrival that a much bigger army was needed and persuaded Manuel to go to Paris and London in person to plead his cause.

Charles welcomed Manuel warmly, even redecorating an entire wing of the old Louvre for him to stay in with his entourage, but, after the disaster at Nicopolis, refused to contemplate another full-blown international crusade.

Manuel then crossed the Channel to England, where Henry the Fourth also treated him with reverence and respect, on Christmas Day entertaining him with a banquet and a joust at his palace in Eltham just outside south-east London, but was also unable to send military aid. He showed genuine sympathy for the Byzantine plight, however, and on Manuel's departure handed him £4,000 that had been contributed to the church collection boxes set up across England specifically for the purpose.

Ironically, twenty-one years later, the instigator of the allied effort, le Maingre, as a prisoner of war for the second time, died in captivity in Yorkshire after fighting in the French vanguard at Agincourt.

Meanwhile, Christians had a brief respite from Ottoman depredations when the fratricide Bayezid was confronted by another devout Muslim – Tamerlane. This name was feared throughout Asia, for his horde was known to destroy everything in its path. In 1398 his advance guard and right wing, under a grandson, invaded the Punjab. The left wing, under another grandson, marched by way of Lahore. He himself, with a small, picked force, traversed the highest regions of the Hindu Kush before turning south to join his main body east of the Indus. Killing and plundering, he marched towards Delhi. On the way he won the Battle of Panipat, after which he massacred 100,000 captive Indian soldiers, which took several horrible days. Then he stormed Delhi, his men slaughtering, raping, plundering and destroying. He next marched north into the Himalayan foothills, storming supposedly impregnable Meerut, then westward back to the Punjab, destroying everything on the way. Then he disappeared from India as suddenly as he came, returning to his hometown of Samarkand with a fabulous booty.

In 1400 he invaded Armenia and Georgia. Of the surviving populations, more than 60,000 were taken as slaves, and many districts were depopulated. He then turned his attention to Syria, where he beat a Mamluke army at the Battle of Aleppo. He captured both Aleppo and Damascus, slaughtering all the inhabitants except the artisans, who were deported to Samarkand to work as slaves. Then he invaded Iraq.

After the capture of Baghdad, 20,000 of its citizens were massacred. He ordered that every soldier should return with at least two severed human heads to show him. Many warriors were so scared they killed prisoners captured earlier in the campaign just to ensure they had heads to present to him. Those who had no prisoners to kill beheaded their own wives.

Even in his 60s Tamerlane lost none of his ferocious energy. But, despite years of insulting letters passing between him and Bayezid, nothing warranted a war with the Ottomans until Bayezid demanded tribute from an emir loyal to Tamerlane, and Tamerlane took umbrage. He advanced through east Anatolia, capturing the town of Sivas from the Ottomans. After he moved his army again, in the summer of 1402, to just north of Ankara, Bayezid reluctantly withdrew his forces from the blockade of Constantinople and had them march in scorching heat to meet it. When they arrived they were tired and thirsty and had no time to recuperate.

Historical sources exaggerated the number of troops to unrealistic proportions. Contemporary writer and traveller Ahmad ibn Arabshah wrote that Tamerlane had 800,000 troops, which is absurd. Still it was undoubtedly a big army. Tamerlane in fact probably had about 140,000 men and nearly as many horses, as most of the troops would have been cavalry, and it is reliably recorded that he had thirty-two elephants. And this army heavily outnumbered Bayezid's, a quarter of which was recently conquered Mongols.

Bayezid's generals advised him to take up defensive positions and then when Tamerlane's troops pushed back the Ottomans to withdraw into the nearby mountains and force Tamerlane to hunt them in their own terrain in the intense heat. Bayezid instead chose to take an offensive stance and marched eastward. His scouts found no trace of the Timurids, who had secretly marched south-west, had rested and were now encamped to the rear of the Ottomans, in the same locations that the Ottomans had previously occupied, making use of abandoned equipment and tents.

The battle began with a large-scale Ottoman attack countered by swarms of arrows from the Timurid horse archers that killed several thousand. Many surrendered. Also, Bayezid had made the fundamental mistake of placing his Mongol cavalry in the vanguard. Unwilling to fight fellow Mongols, they deserted and went over to the enemy. During the battle Tamerlane diverted a creek, the main water supply of both armies, to an off-stream reservoir, depriving the Ottomans of water. The Ottoman forces, exhausted, deserted, betrayed by allies and now also parched, stood no chance. Within a couple of hours 15,000 of them lay dead. Though Bayezid fled to the mountains with a few hundred horsemen, Tamerlane had the mountains surrounded and he was soon captured and led in chains to the victor's tent.

Some accounts say that as Tamerlane advanced through Anatolia he had Bayezid carried in front of him in an iron cage, occasionally using him as a pouffe and as a stool to mount his horse, that he took over the sultan's *harem* for his own personal use and forced Bayezid's Serbian wife to serve naked at his table, but all this is more generally regarded as a myth. Among the descriptions of contemporaries and witnesses of the events, the only mention of a cage and other humiliation is in the works of ibn Arabshah, who wrote that 'Bayezid's heart was broken to pieces' when he saw that his wives and concubines were serving at a banquet, adding that he 'became a prey and was locked up like a bird in a cage'. Modern historian on orientalism H.A.R. Gibb, an editor of the *Encyclopaedia of Islam*, wrote however that this is just a 'flowery style, not a real cage'. He added, 'The flowery elegance of style has also affected historiography.' Bayezid died in captivity, maybe by suicide but indeed possibly of a broken heart, but not at the humiliation of his womenfolk, rather at the loss of his sultanate.

Tamerlane overran all of Anatolia and sacked the Ottoman capital. He reached the Aegean coast, where he besieged and took the town of Smyrna, a stronghold of the Knights of St John, leaving it a smouldering ruin, before returning home to Samarkand and dying of fever as he set out to invade China.

Scholars have calculated that his campaigns caused the deaths of seventeen million people. He rampaged, massacred and destroyed on an unprecedented scale for no reason whatsoever. No more senseless, bloody or devastating campaigns have ever been fought. He converted no one, built nothing and left nobody in place to run the conquered regions. Syria never fully recovered from the devastation.

Though he created nothing but vast wastelands, this nihilism meant the Ottomans' infrastructure remained in place and they recovered. Five sons of Bayezid fought for control of the realm in the Ottoman interregnum of 1402-1413, a power struggle fraught with danger for all involved, as fratricide was a traditional policy in Ottoman succession, the murder of inconvenient princes a Muslim habit. The successful son became Sultan Mehmed the First.

In 1416 uprisings posed a serious challenge to his authority. They erupted in part because he debased the Ottoman silver coinage in which the janissaries received their pay. Although they were all eventually stifled, the series of co-ordinated revolts instigated by an influential mystic, scholar and theologian named Bedreddin and his disciples was suppressed only after great difficulty and massacres of thousands of rebels. Bedreddin was apprehended by Mehmed's forces and executed in a market-place.

Mehmed then concentrated on re-uniting the Ottoman empire and governing his Balkan provinces. The appropriation of Gallipoli having given the Ottomans the bridgehead they needed, they spread across Thrace. After capturing Adrianople in east Thrace they transferred their capital there. In every town and village they captured, most of the population was transported, its place being taken by Turkomen colonists.

One of Mehmed's sons became Sultan Murad the Second when aged only 16, his reign notable for the completion of the conquest of Thessalonica and yet another unsuccessful siege of Constantinople. When Murad II, who was obese, died young of apoplexy at a feast, his widow went to his 19-year-old son Mehmed and congratulated him on his succession as Mehmed the Second. He received her warmly; when she returned to the *harem* she found that her infant son had been murdered in his bath. Mehmed II was taking no chances.

After murdering the toddler, Mehmed cheerfully swore to Emperor Constantine's envoys that he wished to live at peace with Byzantium. But in the summer of 1451, in only five months, he built a strong fortress on the Bosporus a few miles up from Constantinople where the channel was at its narrowest that gave him complete control of the Bosporus and also provided an ideal base from which Constantinople could be attacked from the north-east. Never before had so strong a fortress been built so quickly. Even elderly viziers, muddy-handed and covered with lime-dust, had to roll stones and mix mortar. The emperor sent two successive ambassadors, laden with gifts, with instructions to remind Mehmed that he was breaking his oath and to implore him to at least spare the neighbouring Byzantine villages. Both were sent back without even the courtesy of an audience with the sultan. Constantine made one last effort. These envoys were immediately executed.

When the new fortress was finished, Mehmed issued a proclamation that every passing vessel, no matter what its nationality or provenance, must halt for examination. Late in November, Antonio Rizzo, the skipper of a Venetian galley coming from the Black Sea, ignored the instruction. His galley was blasted by just one huge stone fired by a new fearsome gun. Rizzo and his crew were captured and executed. His corpse was hung on a stake near the fortress, while the limbs of his crew lay scattered and rotting on the ground. Mehmed spared only four men, whom he sent to Constantinople to tell of what had happened, deterring any more ships from attempting to come from the Black Sea.

The gun had been made by an iron founder from Hungary named Orban who had initially offered his services to the Byzantines to build a giant cannon but they could not afford his fee, nor did they have the materials necessary for constructing such a big gun, so he then approached the Ottomans, claiming that his weapon could blast 'the walls of Babylon itself'. He was given abundant funds and materials and built the giant gun in three months.

In January, all over Asia dervishes and Islamic teachers wandered from village to village informing everyone that the sultan would soon besiege Constantinople. He planned to march from Adrianople, the Ottoman capital 140 miles east of Constantinople, after assembling a greater army than any of his ancestors. He thought himself another Alexander the Great. More and more of the great guns were being cast in Adrianople.

Meanwhile, Constantinople prepared for defence, receiving a boost when a big warship from Genoa berthed in the harbour with 700 seasoned men-at-arms on board. Their equipment was impeccable. They carried two-handed swords and wore plate-armour. Accustomed to stern discipline, they respected their commander, a Genoese aristocrat named Giovanni Longo, a renowned expert on siege warfare who had fitted them out and fetched them at his own expense. Despite his appearance – florid, paunchy and puffy around the eyes – he was an experienced professional soldier. Everybody celebrated the arrival of his private army. Seven hundred trained, battle-hardened men well-accoutred in plate armour! Each one was equal to ten of the expendable Muslim irregulars, the lightly-armed, largely untrained *bashi-bazouks* in buff coats who would make the initial assault.

At last the young new sultan, at the age of only 21, stunned his ministers by announcing all was ready. After four failed attempts by Muslim predecessors, the sieges of 674-8, 717, 1391-9 and 1422, Constantinople seemed an impregnable stronghold.

Water protected it from attack on three sides, a natural moat that linked the Black Sea in the north to the Aegean in the south. The city, on the easternmost tip of a broad, triangular promontory, was washed on its south side by the Marmara Sea, which had two long and narrow straits – the Bosporus (the Ox-ford) in the east and the Dardanelles, called in antiquity the Hellespont, in the west. An inlet, the Golden Horn, extended the waterway along the city's north-east, providing a magnificent natural harbour. Constantinople needed major fortification only on its landward west. On the opposite northern shore of the Golden Horn was the town of Pera, a Genoese colony. Its merchants did profitable trade with the Ottomans, and the town planned to remain neutral in the coming conflict.

Mehmed II had been born and raised in Adrianople, where his religious tutors had inculcated in him the imperative of fulfilling his Islamic duty to overthrow the Byzantine empire by conquering Constantinople. The existence of an independent Constantinople controlled and peopled by Christians so close to the Ottomans' capital and right in the centre of their empire that by then stretched from the Danube to the Euphrates was intolerable. Obviously, it had no right to exist all the while its citizens were neither Muslim nor paying *jizya*, any more than had all the territories already conquered. Byzantium was so enfeebled by then that its capital could have been regarded as an irrelevant rotting anachronism. But its very existence, in whatever condition, rankled with Mehmed. To him, its very presence was an insult to Islam, an affront to Allah.

In Constantinople was the *kizil elma*, the 'red apple', symbol of universal sovereignty. This resplendent metal ball, held by the hand in the statue of Emperor Justinian in front of the Church of Hagia Sophia, was the lucky charm of the Byzantine empire. Its capture would symbolise the fulfilment of the Muslims' destiny, the defeat of Christianity and the realisation of their dream of world domination.

Recently, it had been expedient to leave Constantinople as a free port and point of contact with Europe for Muslim merchants. In a humiliating arrangement, a whole area of the city had been set aside for them. They were no longer subject to Byzantine law. Their affairs were regulated by a Muslim *kadi*, a judge. Mehmed opined that this arrangement, though valuable for the purpose of humbling Christians, had now outlasted its usefulness.

Two months after his meeting with his ministers, even they were astonished at the size of the Ottoman armada that assembled off Gallipoli; as were the Byzantines when it dropped anchor near Constantinople. Meanwhile, Mehmed had also gathered in Thrace a colossal army of 100,000 men. But even that was not all. There was also the giant gun. Sixty oxen in pairs dragged it to Constantinople, with 200 men holding it steady, after another 200 men had been sent out to pave the way, smoothing the roads and strengthening the bridges. Orban also sent other cannon for the Muslims, smaller but still powerful. Everything was in place for a prolonged siege.

The great Finnish novelist Miko Waltari described the siege in *The Dark Angel* after consulting the diary of an eyewitness, a Venetian physician named Niccolò Barbaro, kept in the Nazionale Marciana library in Venice. *The Dark Angel*, published in 1952 and translated into English the following year by Naomi Walford, is also written in the form of a diary. The narrator is a man aged 40 named John Angelos who has returned to Constantinople, the city of his birth, though he was brought up in Avignon, travelled much and lived for several years in Florence, to help lead the defenders.

They were made up of Greeks and what he calls 'Latins'. The city was wholly under the control of the Latins, and the Greeks had no power, although the emperor seemed not to have realised this. The harbour was held by Latin vessels, and the key points of the city and its walls were manned by Venetians and Longo's iron-clad Genoese troops. Angelos's father was Greek and Angelos feels inclined to mix more with the Greek soldiers than with the Latins, though he spends much time also with Longo.

In his journal entry of 9 March he describes the digging of a moat:

To-day the great galleys were rowed into Kynegion Harbour, with pennants fluttering, horns bellowing and drums rumbling. Seamen and soldiers came ashore in good order, and having been given picks, shovels and baskets, were marched off in parties, under their own standards; they passed out through the wall by the Hebdomon Palace. Here Emperor Constantine, dressed in purple and gold, awaited them on horseback, and bade them welcome.

The ditch, which is to be a good hundred paces long, was already measured and marked out, and the ships' captains thrust their standards into the ground at the points allotted them. It was to be eight feet wide and eight feet deep: an easy enough task for close on two thousand men. At a sign from the emperor, waiting servants broached scores of wine-jars, whereupon each man might go and pour himself a measure of wine. Little wonder, then, if they set to work singing, and vied with one another in digging and in filling the baskets, which others carried off at the run for the reinforcement of the outer wall. It was a fine sight, and many people gathered to watch. The presence of the emperor spurred even captains, mates and shipowners to bear a hand. By dusk the work was complete. Certainly this ditch is not to be compared with the great ditch or moat whose walls are bricked, though the sides of this one too are to be revetted with stones and timber.

On 15 March he writes:

When the training-exercises were resumed, we fired off a heavy cannon from the top of the wall. Longo wanted to accustom the recruits to the noise, flash and smoke, to prove to them that gunfire is more alarming than dangerous, as he himself believes. The emperor's German technician Johann Grant had mounted the gun as firmly as possible on the wall; it fired according to calculations, hurling a stone ball the size of a man's head in a high arc over the outer wall and the ditch, and fell, shaking the ground. But the great wall shook more. A long crack ran up it and big stones fell to the ground; and although no one was hurt, the incident confirmed what Longo had said; that cannon are more dangerous for those who use them than for the enemy. It had a depressing effect, and monks and artisans stared at the fissure unwilling to believe their eyes, for it showed them how illusory was the impregnability of that massive wall.

The drawbridge has not yet been destroyed, so I ordered the partly-blocked gate to be opened, and sent a few men out to retrieve the cannon-ball. Even the most able stonemason needs at least a day to shape hard stone into a ball of given diameter. I placed archers on the turrets and behind the crenellations of the outer wall, just as if we were making a real sortie. The men I sent out felt unprotected, and glanced about in fear as soon as they left the shelter of the ramparts. But they soon plucked up courage, went out and dug up the ball, and brought it back with them.

The Muslim army's vanguard arrived on 1 April, Easter Day, by which time a mighty boom had been completed across the Golden Horn preventing Muslim ships from sailing up it to the port, the chain winding like a huge serpent from shore to shore.

Angelos describes it:

The round-hewn timbers that are to keep the chain at surface-level are so massive that a grown man cannot get his arms round some of them. The links are made of iron as thick as my calf, and if placed on end would reach halfway up my thigh. The baulks of timber are fastened end to end with huge hooks. The famous boom placed by the Knights of St John across the entrance to Rhodes harbour is a toy to this. Not the mightiest vessel could break through it.

On 4 April he describes the defenders' weapons:

Numbers of culverins have been placed on the battlements, also some heavy bombards, which spew forth their mighty stone balls in a lofty arch. But the bombards have not yet been tested; the powder is being saved for the muskets and swivel-guns which fire leaden bullets. The emperor's technicians have also erected old-fashioned ballistas and catapults. These hurl great boulders far across the ditch, though the missiles travel more slowly than those of the bombards. Where there is a choice between handgun and crossbow, only one man in fifty will choose the gun. The crossbow is both surer and safer.

Shortly after dawn on the next day he joins Greek cavalry in a sortie. He writes:

A cloud of dust began rising from all the roads and tracks leading to the city. Through it appeared scattered Muslim troops. When they saw the walls they began calling upon Allah and brandishing their weapons. Spear-points and scimitars flashed redly through the dust.

In well-dressed ranks the Greeks rode forth, but while yet on the drawbridge they set spurs to their mounts and tore off at full gallop, each striving to be first. I followed over the thundering ground. My great steed was furious at being left behind, accustomed as he was to careering ahead of all the rest; he did his utmost, therefore, and I felt as safe as if I had been on the back of a war-elephant, in a timber *howdah*.

We rode straight at a detachment of infantry who were approaching along the road from Adrianople. When these troops saw us they opened out on either side of the road; then the first of their arrows sang towards us. The young Greeks also deployed, as if they had been playing ball, each of them aiming at a Turkish head. Then my charger trod the first corpse underfoot. Far away on one flank a troop of Turkish *spahis* [the French form of a Persian name for light cavalry] in fluttering red cloaks were advancing at a gallop.

The first of the Turks had thrown away their weapons in their fright, so as to be able to run more swiftly. Then a group closed their ranks, lowered their pikes and thrust them into the ground to halt our horses. The Greeks swerved to encircle the troop, but my stallion blundered straight in among the spears, snapped them off like sticks against his breastplate and trampled the terrified Turks underfoot.

I had come to fight, and fight I must. But these men had not even buff jerkins. The field was strewn with bundles of ragged clothes. My horse put his ears back and sank his teeth in the belly of a young Turk, shook the life out of him and tossed him aside.

The Turkish columns had halted in disorder. The Greeks swung their horses' heads about and rode off, until they came to rising ground and had to slacken speed. Arrows were still whistling among us, though as yet no one had fallen from the saddle.

We turned back towards the city. As we rode past wounded Turks writhing on the ground with their hands to their heads, one or another of the young Greeks, by way of practice, bent and delivered the *coup de grâce*.

The air was heavy with the stench of blood and excrement. From some way off the *spahis* approached us in wild career, invoking Allah and brandishing their scimitars in flashing arcs. They rolled towards us like a red, tempestuous wave, and more and more of our young men looked behind them and furtively spurred on their steeds.

I did not look round. I kept my gaze fixed upon the walls and bastions of Constantinople rising before me. I tried to see them through Turkish eyes, and could not wonder that their infantry had halted at the sight of them. They extended as far as the eye could

Desert encampment. (*Photo © Wellcome Collection*)

Charles Martel defeating the Muslims near Paris. (*Photo © Wikimedia Commons*)

The plague in Germany in the 14th century. (*Photo © Wellcome Collection*)

A Janissary chief. (*Photo © Wellcome Collection*)

Muslim slave traders take their captives to Timbuktu. (*Photo © Mary Evans Picture Library*)

Original Assassins are furtively lectured by Islamic scholars on a street corner. (*Photo © Mary Evans Picture Library*)

Ottoman sultan Murad I. (*Photo © Mary Evans Picture Library*)

Tamerlane. (*Photo © Mary Evans Picture Library*)

Draculea. (*Photo © Mary Evans Picture Library*)

Dome of the Rock shrine in Jerusalem. (*Photo © Mary Evans Picture Library*)

Richard the Lionheart fights Saladin. (*Photo © Mary Evans Picture Library*)

Evil sultan Mehmed II dying and Satan taking his soul. (*Photo © Mary Evans Picture Library*)

Siege of Rhodes 1522. (*Photo © Adobe Stock*)

Siege of Szeged 1556, where Suleiman the Magnificent died of excitement at victory. (*Photo © Mary Evans Picture Library*)

Great Siege of Malta 1565. (*Photo © Mary Evans Picture Library*)

La Valette at the Great Siege. (*Photo © Mary Evans Picture Library*)

Barbary pirates with captives. (*Photo © Wellcome Collection*)

Cervantes, wounded hero at Battle of Lepanto. (*Photo © Adobe Stock*)

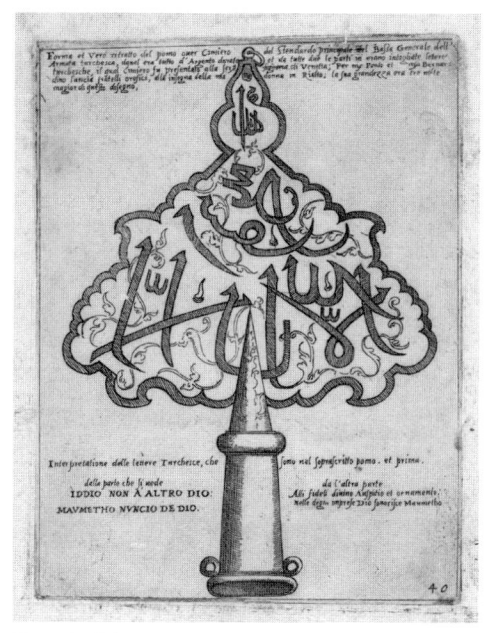

Finial of Ottoman standard at Lepanto, with tenets of Islam. (*Photo © Wellcome Collection*)

Siege of Vienna 1683. The assault of the janissaries from the castle bastion. On the left stands the iron-willed Ernst Rüdiger von Starhemberg, the garrison commander. (*Photo © Mary Evans Picture Library*)

Helmet of Jan Sobieski. The wings denote he was commander of the famed and fearsome Polish winged hussars, the saviours of European culture and civilisation. (*Photo © Mary Evans Picture Library*)

Paintings of the fall of Constantinople. (*Photo © Adobe Stock*)

Paintings of the fall of Constantinople. (*Photo © Adobe Stock*)

Paintings of the fall of Constantinople. (*Photo © Adobe Stock*)

reach, those yellow and brown, castellated, turreted ramparts. First came the ditch with its counterscarp; beyond it the first low outworks, then the outer wall with its towers, garrison and artillery, this wall alone being mightier than any city wall I had seen in Europe. Yet behind that again, loftier than the tallest house, rose the great wall of Constantinople with its massive bastions. Outworks, outer wall and great wall looked like three gigantic steps. Even should the enemy succeed in surmounting the first two, they would still be penned in a death-trap between the second and third.

As I beheld these towering steps I felt for the first time a glimmer of hope. Nothing short of an earthquake could breach those walls, I thought.

Then my horse was trotting across the resounding drawbridge. The line of *spahis* with their plumes, breastplates and floating cloaks had halted a bowshot to our rear. Hardly had we regained the city before the engineers raced out to tear down the bridge, while masons stood ready with bricks and mortar to wall up the gateway. In the same way the four last drawbridges were demolished and the last gateways bricked up. All that remained were the narrow sally-ports in the great wall.

Later that day Mehmed himself arrived. By then the whole north-west horizon was lit by the glow of the Muslim troops' campfires, and when the soldiers prostrated themselves for noon prayers a huge, living carpet seemed to cover the earth from the shores of the Marmara to the innermost end of the Golden Horn. From all directions the Muslims continued their advance, deployed and halted out of range. Great herds of cattle were driven along behind them. On the other side of the Horn, too, endless marching columns appeared. By evening the Muslims were massed so densely from the inner end of the Horn to the Marmara that a rabbit could not have slipped through them. But they halted 2,000 yards away from the city and to the defenders on the walls they looked the size of ants.

The next day the Muslims dug a trench beyond the range of the city's artillery, and placed stones and erected palisades to protect their camp. Angelos writes:

A few janissaries ran up to our defenders and challenged them to single combat. The officers of the emperor's guard eagerly begged leave to go down and display their skill in arms, and among Longo's men too there were some who would gladly have matched the western two-handed sword against the short, curved blades of the janissaries, but Longo sternly forbade rashness.

'The age of tournaments is past,' he said. 'A brave soldier serves no good purpose by risking his life in a foolish contest of honour. I was summoned here to wage war, not to play games.'

He ordered his best marksmen to take aim with arquebus and crossbow and fire a volley. Five janissaries fell, struck by bullets and bolts. The rest, enraged by this breach of honourable convention, foamed at the mouth and cursed the defenders for cowardly wretches who dared not tackle brave men save from the shelter of their walls. After two more had fallen the remainder came to their senses and tried to carry back their comrades' bodies. By now firing was general all along the wall, and many fell. But fresh janissaries came in unbroken succession, heedless of missiles, to remove the corpses. Not one body was left by the ditch; nothing remained but a few bloodstains on the grass.

There then came from the direction of the island of Selymbria occasional rumbling as of thunder, though the sky was clear. From the island in the Marmara a mighty pillar of smoke was rising to the sky. The Muslims' fleet had for two days been vainly trying to storm this last island stronghold. Now wood had been stacked round the tower and set alight, and most of the garrison were burnt alive inside. Forty escaped the fire but were captured, and that night their naked, mutilated corpses swarming with flies were impaled on stakes outside Constantinople's Selymbrian Gate.

The next day Angelos and Longo viewed from the battlements the giant gun. No one had ever seen before such a mighty piece of ordnance. Protected by a ditch and a palisade, it had been placed opposite the Kaligari Gate, where the wall was thickest. Longo was curious to see this piece, and since all was quiet he allowed Angelos to go with him. Angelos writes:

Hulagu and Baybars; Othman founds the Ottoman empire

Many of the garrison had left their posts and gathered in big groups to look at the giant bombard, while townspeople too had climbed onto palace roofs and towers for a better view of the monster.

Some pointed and shouted that they recognised Orban, although he was wearing a Turkish *kaftan* of honour and the headdress of Master of the Ordnance. The Greeks showered curses and abuse, and the emperor's technicians took aim with swivel-gun and arquebus, firing several rounds to disturb the Turks at their laborious task of raising and mounting the great gun.

The emperor's technician, Johann Grant, also joined us. It was the first time I had met this remarkable man, of whose skill and attainments I had heard so much. He is middle-aged with a black beard; his forehead is furrowed with thought and his gaze restless and searching. He was pleased to find that I knew a few words of German, though he speaks fluent Latin and has already learnt a good deal of Greek. The emperor took him into his service as a successor to Orban, and pays him the salary that Orban begged for in vain.

Grant said, 'That gun is a marvel of the founder's art, exceeding anything we believed possible. The emperor's technicians and I have worked out and proved, for our own amusement, that so large a cannon cannot be cast satisfactorily – and that if one could cast it, it would not hold together. And supposing even that it could be fired, it would only spit the ball a few yards.'

The next day, when the giant gun is fired for the first time Grant is proved wrong. Angelos graphically describes the event:

From the battlements we saw the sultan coming to inspect his largest cannon. He halted prudently at a distance from it of five hundred paces. All the horses were then led away.

Even the Turkish gunners fled from the great bombard, leaving only a half-naked slave waving the smouldering match on a long linstock to make it blaze.

Then came a flash, and a roar more frightful than the loudest thunderclap. The wall shook as if from an earthquake; I lost my balance and fell, like many others. A mighty smoke-cloud, black as gunpowder, hid the bombard from us. I heard later that in nearby houses plates had fallen from the tables and water in the jars slopped over. Even the ships in the harbour trembled.

As soon as the wind had borne away the smoke and the dust from the wall I saw the Turkish gunners running up to look, and to point out to each other the effect of the shot. I saw them shout and wave their arms but heard nothing; the din had deafened me. I shouted myself, but no one heard. Only by pulling at the sleeves of one or two dazed arbalesters could I get them to draw their crossbows. But in their agitation they shot wildly; not one Turk was injured, though many of our men were firing at them from loopholes and embrasures.

The enemy gunners were so spellbound that they cast only vague, fleeting glances at the arrows that were stabbing into the ground about them, as they slowly returned to their gun conversing and shaking their heads, seemingly dissatisfied with what they had seen.

The mighty stone ball had merely made a hollow in the wall, hardly as big as a small room, and had naturally been smashed into a thousand pieces. But the foundations of the wall remained unshaken.

Over by the bombard I saw Orban swinging his club of office and bawling orders. A group of soldiers swarmed round the gun, wrapping it in thick woollen blankets that the metal might not cool too quickly, and pouring oil by the barrelful into its vast maw, to ease its recovery after the terrific strain of the discharge.

Sultan Mehmed alone remained erect when all his suite flung themselves on the ground at the detonation. He was standing motionless now, staring at the ramparts, while his officers brushed the dust from their clothes. He stood still because he did not wish to betray his feelings. Perhaps in his own mind he had half-fancied that a single shot from so mighty a weapon could indeed bring down a twenty-foot wall.

When Orban had seen to it that the great gun was snugly covered, the other two cannon on either side were discharged. They are powerful enough, yet they look like piglets beside the great mother sow. The gunner touched them off without seeking cover. Nevertheless, the two flashes following close upon one another dazzled me for a moment, and the view was hidden by the pitchy clouds of smoke that billowed up and followed the missiles. The stone balls struck at almost the same point as the first, sending a tremor through the wall, and through the rising dust-cloud whirled a rain of stone splinters. A Venetian was wounded by some of these.

But while the Turks tended their guns as if they had been sick cattle, Grant set the whole garrison to work. Knowing now on what point the enemy guns were trained, he caused huge leather bags stuffed with wool, cotton and grass to be lowered, to protect the holes in the outer face of the wall. He was cheerful and was of the opinion that the damage could easily be made good during the night.

Soon fresh rumblings were to be heard and the wall quaked under my feet, for now the sultan's hundreds of slender culverins and serpentines opened fire, and his short, stocky mortars hurled their stones in lofty arcs. Many of the missiles flew over the walls into the city and brought down a few houses before the gunners learned to estimate the correct charge and to lay the guns at the proper angle. The air was filled with incessant din, and scattered parties of Turks began to advance towards the ditch, clashing brass plates together and praising Allah at the tops of their voices. But up on the walls the defenders were growing accustomed to the firing and took good aim, so that many Turks fell by the moat and their comrades suffered losses as they retired with the dead.

I set off for the parapet of the outer wall near the Gate of St Romanus, to tell Longo that so far the great gun had proved less formidable than had been expected.

Cooling, swabbing, laying and reloading the gun takes nearly three hours. (The cooling is done with copious amounts of olive oil bought from Genoese merchants in Pera, causing a shortage in Constantinople.) Meanwhile, the Muslims fire conventional cannon as before, though even these are bigger and more powerful than normal.

Angelos is by the Romanus Gate when one of these guns is fired in that direction. 'Part of the battlements of the outer wall collapsed and countless splinters sang through the air,' he writes. 'Lime dust choked me and the poisonous smoke blackened my hands and face. Close beside me a hapless unarmoured workman, carrying stone for the walls, fell headlong, blood pouring from his torn side, dying instantly.

'Again the walls trembled under our feet, a roar shook heaven and earth, and the air was darkened. The giant bombard had been fired a second time. No other noise can compare with it. The sun glowed like a red ball through the cloud of dust and smoke. I estimated that it had taken about two hours to cool, swab, lay and load this great gun.

'Two rounds from the heavy Turkish guns had demolished the breastworks and damaged the outer wall. Indeed, at one or two points it was cracked from top to bottom. Longo roared at the frightened workmen to carry away their comrade's body. These peaceful artisans were crouching in the passage between the outer and main walls, crying to be let into the city through the sally-port. At last two of them crawled up on to the outer wall, knelt by the body and wept to see the wounds inflicted upon it by the stone splinters. With dirty, clumsy hands they brushed the lime-dust from the dead man's face and beard, and felt his chilling limbs as if unable to believe that a man could die so suddenly.'

On 13 April Angelos writes, 'An unquiet night. Not many in the city have slept. At midnight the ground shook again from the detonation of the great gun, and the mighty flash from its muzzle lit the sky. All night men worked at repairing the cracks in the wall and facing the threatened points with sacks of wool and hay.'

The next day he writes, 'Today one of the great Turkish cannon exploded, and smoke poured from cracks in the barrel. The bombardment has slackened. The Turks have set up forges beside the gun-emplacements, and are strengthening the weapons with bands of iron. Orban has established a foundry on the hillside behind the Turkish camp, and at night a red glow mounts from it into the sky. Tin- and copper-smelting continues throughout the twenty-four hours.'

On 17 April, two hours after dusk in a surprise first assault, the Muslims tried to storm the outer wall opposite the Romanus Gate.

Under cover of darkness they crept forward to the moat and laid scaling-ladders across it. If the garrison had not been at work repairing the day's damage the attack might have succeeded. But now the alarm was given in time; trumpets sounded on the walls, pitch-torches were lit and the attackers retreated. Angelos writes:

> After the failure of this surprise attack, drums great and small thundered in the Turkish lines and the assailants raised a fearful yell which could be heard across the city. With long hooks they began pulling down the temporary breastworks and destroying what they could, and at the same time they tried to set fire to the sacks of hay and wool hanging along the wall. The battle lasted four hours without a break. The Turks approached the walls at other points as well, but the main attack was directed at Longo's sector.
>
> In the night darkness the noise and tumult seemed doubly terrible, and people in the city fled half-naked from their houses. As I hastened to join Longo I caught sight of Emperor Constantine, and he was weeping because he fancied the city already lost.
>
> In fact, only a few Turks came even as far as the top of the outer wall. There they were at once cut down by Longo's men, who, like a living, moving wall of iron, barred their way. The scaling-ladders were thrust off with long poles as soon as raised, while seething pitch and molten lead were slopped from great ladles upon the assailants below. The enemy suffered heavy losses and by morning their dead lay in heaps in front of the wall. Among these were only a few janissaries, from which it was evident that for this attempt the sultan had sent in only the less efficient of his light troops.
>
> Nevertheless, when the Turks retired many of Longo's men were so exhausted that they sank down where they stood, and slept. Constantine, who inspected the wall shortly after the battle, had to shake many of the sentries with his own hand, to rouse them. Longo forced the Greek workmen to descend into the ditch and clear it of all the material with which the Turks had sought to fill it. Many went to their deaths in this way, when the enemy in revenge for their failure discharged their cannon in the dark.

The mood of the townsfolk is one of hope and enthusiasm, for the successful repulse has cheered us all. And Longo has spread exaggerated accounts of the Turkish losses. But to me he said bluntly, 'We must not be puffed up over a victory that was no victory. The attack was an ordinary reconnaissance to test the strength of the wall. A thousand men at most took part in it, as I've learnt from our prisoners. But custom requires me to issue a communiqué. So, when I put it about that we have beaten off a heavy attack, that the Turks have lost ten thousand men killed and as many wounded, while our own losses are confined to one man killed and a sprained ankle, every seasoned soldier knows what it means and pays no heed. But on the city's morale it will have an excellent effect.' He looked at me with a smile and added, 'You fought bravely and well.'

'Did I? There was such confusion that I hardly knew what I was doing.'

This was true. This morning I found my sword sticky with blood but the events of the night I recalled only as a muddled nightmare.

I have visited the wounded, who lie on straw in empty stables and sheds near the wall. The experienced Latin warriors have set aside money for surgeons, and are therefore receiving expert care, but the Greeks are tended only by a few trained nuns, who do it purely out of charity.

On 20 April three Genoese galleys with reinforcements sent by the pope arrived off the Hellespont, where they were joined by a heavy transport made available by Alfonso of Aragon with a cargo of corn from Sicily. The sultan immediately rode around the head of the Golden Horn to send his orders personally to his admiral, Suleiman Baltoglu. On no account were the reinforcements or corn to reach the city.

In the city there was great excitement when the four Christian ships were sighted. With bellying canvas they sailed steadily in over a heavy swell, amid a turmoil of Muslim galleys. The big merchant vessel had hoisted the purple pendant of the emperor.

Angelos stands on the high wall facing the sea among a group of breathless, waving, shouting townsfolk. He writes:

The vessels were already so near that the wind carried to us the noise of battle – shouts, oaths and shots. The Turkish flagship had rammed the largest vessel amidships and was fast in her side. To each of the others Turkish galleys had made fast with hooks and grapnels, so that the mighty ships trailed a bunch of light craft along with them.

All about me excitedly yelling people were telling how the battle had started far out to sea. The sultan himself had ridden out into the shallow water near the Marmara Tower to call orders to his vessels and urge the captains to destroy the Christian fleet. It was said that he had bared his teeth like a dog and foamed at the mouth.

Slowly, but steadily, the wind drove the great ships towards the harbour and safety, dragging the Turkish galleys with them as a bear drags hounds clinging to its coat. There were so many of the enemy craft that they often collided with one another, and the great waves were topped with bloody foam. Now and then one of the galleys gave up the struggle, cast off and pulled away to make room for another. Far out to sea drifted a single foundering galley.

The air was full of the din of drums and horns, hideous shrieks and dying howls. In the water floated corpses and wreckage. On their lofty decks Christians in plate-armour, wielding axes, swords, and pikes, fought off the Turks who continually swarmed up the steep sides of the ships. The Turkish admiral stood on the quarter-deck of his galley with a speaking-trumpet, roaring his orders.

Someone recognised the captain of the ship that flew the imperial pendant. This vessel had sailed for Sicily before the siege, to fetch grain. On board of her could be plainly seen the captain, a giant of a man who grimaced, laughed, brandished a bloodstained battle-axe and pointed out to his archers the enemy perched aloft in the rigging of the galleys.

The Genoese had wetted their sails, that the fiery arrows might not set them alight. But across the deck of an enemy galley there suddenly spurted a stream of fire, and the shrieks of the burnt Turks for a moment drowned the noise of battle. The damaged vessel withdrew from the conflict, leaving behind her a blazing wake.

It was an incredible sight to see these four Christian ships cutting their way irresistibly towards the harbour, surrounded by at least forty Turkish war-galleys. The jubilation of the crowd is not to be described. Again and again they yelled that the papal fleet was on its way and that these were but the forerunners. Constantinople was saved!

The reeking, seething hurly-burly of craft passed Acropolis Point, and here the ships were compelled to alter course to larboard, to make the boom and the Golden Horn. By this they lost the following wind and their steerage way. Under the lee of the high hill the sails hung slack, and it was clear that the vessels no longer answered to the helm. A shout of triumph rose from the Turkish galleys and the watching crowds fell silent. From the hills on the further shore a triumphant yell reached us against the wind. There stood dense masses of Turkish onlookers, praising Allah.

Fighting incessantly, the Christian ships closed up; they would not abandon one another, though the Turkish flagship still had her bows fast in the hull of the largest Genoese and hampered her movements. Grappled to one another, side by side, the four vessels rocked in the swell like a conglomerate fortress, spewing forth stones, roundshot, arrows and molten lead over the Turks. In hissing arches, Greek fire spurted across the enemy decks and kept the crews busy extinguishing it.

The ships were now so near that the faces of the fighting men could be plainly distinguished, but no one could help them. Behind the harbour-boom the Venetians were cleared for action, but the chain prevented them from coming out in support.

Infinitely slowly, inch by inch, the fire-spitting fortress of ships glided towards the boom, laboriously impelled by the sea-swell and a few mighty oars.

Along the wall and on the hills of the city the people fell on their knees to pray. The suspense was now unendurable, so formidable was the Turkish superiority, so doggedly did the galleys relieve one another and come fresh to the fray. Their admiral was hoarse from shouting, and blood poured down his cheek. With severed wrists, the turbaned boarders fell into the sea and drowned, while their hands remained clinging convulsively to the rails of the Christian ships.

And suddenly it was as if a blue puff of wind passed across the sky. Through the air swept a fold of the Virgin's blue robe. A miracle came to pass: the wind changed! The heavy wet sails filled once more and the floating mass moved nearer to the boom. At the last moment, the Turkish admiral ordered his crew to hack away the bows of the flagship, so that only her stem remained wedged in the hull of the Christian. With blood pouring from the scuppers, he turned his galley and rowed away. Limping, with smashed oars, smothered in smoke from the unquenchable Greek fire, the rest of the Turkish craft followed their commander, and the continuous cheering of the people of Constantinople shook the very heavens.

I know little of miracles; but that the wind should change just at that decisive moment seemed little less. There was something holy in the event, something which the human senses could not grasp. Nor was its strangeness dimmed by the shrieks of the wounded or by the seamen's hoarse oaths as with exhausted voices they hailed the harbour, asking for the boom to be opened. To unfasten the great chain is a difficult and dangerous task, and not until the Turkish vessels had vanished up the Bosporus was it allowed to be done; and the four ships staggered into port amid salutes in honour of the emperor.

That same afternoon the ships' companies paraded with their colours, led by their officers and followed by rejoicing crowds, through the city to the Khora church, there to render thanks for their preservation. All the wounded who could walk came too, and some of the others were carried on stretchers to the church in the hope of miraculous healing.

But the reinforcements and corn were too little too late. The winds that prevented Admiral Baltoglu from intercepting them heralded an apocalyptic storm. Hail, driving rain and a torrent of floodwater were so severe that a procession invoking the protection of the Virgin Mary had to be abandoned after the icon slipped to the ground from its platform, causing it to be damaged. In the circumstances, this damage naturally was interpreted as a bad omen.

And confirmation that the Virgin was withholding her protection came immediately. That night the Muslims dragged up more guns and reinforced their batteries and their new method of aiming at separate points along the wall proved successful. In the afternoon of the following day one of the towers near the Romanus Gate collapsed, and with it a large portion of the main wall itself. The breach was considerable. If the attacking force had been stronger they might have penetrated the city, for at the corresponding point in the outer wall there remained only the temporary palisade that had to be renewed every night. But luckily the Muslims had been sending detachments not more than a couple of hundred strong to test different points along the wall. These had now no time to carry off their dead, and so many corpses lay by the outer wall and where the moat had fallen in that the stench of them poisoned the air.

Skirmishes continued all day until late in the evening, the Muslims testing the ramparts at every point. On the high ground they set up more cannon in an attempt to bombard the ships in the harbour. More than 150 cannon balls fell there. When the Venetian ships rowed away from the boom to avoid them, the Muslim galleys tried to break the chain, but the alarm was given in time for the Venetians to return and defend it; they were also able to inflict such damage on the enemy galleys that these made off. During this action the Muslims could not fire for fear of hitting their own ships. Three times the Muslim fleet tried in vain to break through the boom.

Angelos writes:

It is as if the sultan were moving heaven and earth to avenge yesterday's disgraceful defeat at sea. They say that last night he rode out to the Port of Pillars and with his own hand belaboured his admiral on breast and shoulders with the iron club of an emir. Admiral Baltoglu was already severely wounded and had lost an eye in the fighting, and two hundred men aboard his flagship had perished, so that it was all he could do to withdraw from the battle unaided. Without doubt he is a brave man, albeit incapable of commanding a whole fleet; this is evident from yesterday's turmoil.

The sultan meant to impale him, but the seamen and their officers pleaded for him on the grounds of his personal valour; therefore Mehmed confined himself to having him flogged. The man was made to lie face downwards on the ground in front of the whole fleet, and was thrashed with rods until he lost consciousness. All his property has been confiscated and he has been dismissed from the sultan's camp.

The next day was a Sunday. Angelos calls it a Sunday of horror. In the night the Muslims had built what amounted to a railroad around the boom and transported more than fifty galleys by land. Iron wheels and metal tracks had been cast and carpenters had fashioned wooden cradles big enough to accommodate the keels of moderate-sized ships, which were then moved like trains. The vessels had been slowly hauled along the track by innumerable teams of oxen over and along the embankment and then lowered into the water the other side of the boom.

Angelos writes:

This morning the church bells fell silent and on the wall overlooking the harbour great numbers of townsfolk assembled, rubbing their eyes in mute amazement. There was scared talk of sorcery and of dervishes who could walk on the water and use their mantles as sails. Directly opposite the Church of St Nicholas and the Gate of St Theodosias, the Pera harbour is crammed with Turkish galleys. No one could imagine how these vessels had crossed the boom so as to lie as they now do in the rear of ours. Many rubbed their eyes again and vowed that the ships were a hallucination. But the Pera shore was swarming with Turks, who were throwing up earthworks, raising palisades and laying cannon to protect their vessels.

Then a shout went up. On the high ground above, a galley suddenly appeared and began gliding downhill with all sails set, amid the music of drums and trumpets. She seemed to be sailing on dry land. Hauled by hundreds of men along a timber slipway, she moved down to the shore, splashed into the water and freed herself from the timber cradle that had supported her, to be rowed away to join the other ships, of which there was a row of at least fifty. None of these are large, however; they carry eighteen or twenty oars and are between fifty and seventy feet long.

The sultan contrived this surprise manoeuvre in the course of only twenty-four hours. Later it was known that the Genoese in Pera had supplied him with a vast quantity of timber, rope, rollers and lard [sheep and ox tallow] for greasing the slipway. Then with the help of wind-machines, oxen and labourers the Turks hauled the ships from the Bosporus up the steep hill behind Pera, that they might glide down the other side to the Golden Horn.

The Genoese of Pera say in their own defence that everything happened so swiftly and secretly that until dawn this morning they had no inkling of these preparations. As for selling such enormous quantities of lard, their excuse is that to preserve their neutrality they are obliged to trade as much with the sultan as with the city. And even if they had known what was going on they could not have prevented it, for tens of thousands of Turkish warriors are posted on the hill to guard the galleys.

Not only was the defenders' only major harbour no longer secure; they now had more than three miles of extra sea wall to defend.

Constantine knew he could not hold out much longer. Food was running short; more and more of the defenders along the walls were taking time off to find sustenance for their families. In the early hours of 7 May more than 10,000 Muslims stormed the breaches. The heaviest assault was directed at Longo's force by the Romanus Gate, where the great gun had caused the most damage in both walls. Only Longo's presence of mind saved the situation. Angelos writes that Longo, 'bellowing like a bull', hurled himself into the hottest of the fray and with his two-handed sword cut down the foremost Muslims, who had already reached the summit of the earthen rampart. At the same time torches and flares were lit and all was as bright as day.

Angelos continues:

Longo's roars overtopped the shrieks and drumbeats of the Turks, and as soon as he saw that this was to be a full-scale attack he sent word to the reserves. But when the battle had raged for two hours he had to draw further reinforcements from other parts of the wall on either side of the Romanus Gate. After the first attack the Turks returned in regular waves of a thousand at a time. They had dragged their field-pieces right up to the ditch. While the shock troops went in, archers and artillery tried to force the defenders to take cover; but, protected by their plate-armour, Longo's men formed a living wall of iron along the top of the outer rampart. Ladders were thrown down and the Turks who had pressed forward under penthouses to the foot of the wall were showered with boiling pitch and lead until they scattered, exposing themselves to the bolts from the defenders' crossbows.

A gigantic janissary, by sheer bodily strength, scrambled up on the wall and with a yell of triumph called his comrades as he dashed off in pursuit of Longo, the men in armour giving way before him. Longo was fighting in the breach a little lower down and would have fared ill had not one of the workmen, an ordinary Greek without armour, taken a bold leap from the battlements and hewn off one of the janissary's feet with his broad battle-axe. It was then an easy matter for Longo to despatch him. Longo gave his rescuer a handsome reward but said he would rather have dealt with his assailant single-handed.

I witnessed this scene by the light of torches and fire-arrows, amid shrieks and the clash of shields. Then I had no time to think of anything, for the pressure of the attack was so formidable that we had to support one another three deep to withstand it. Today my sword is blunt. When at dawn the Turks began their withdrawal I was so mortally weary that I could hardly lift an arm. Every limb ached and my body was covered with bruises and tender swellings. But I was unwounded and in that respect luckier than many. Longo had been gashed in the armpit by a spear but his armour had prevented fatal harm.

It is hard to estimate the Turkish casualties. Longo launched rumours in the city that at dawn the heaps of the fallen had risen to the height of the outer wall, but this, of course, is nonsense calculated to put heart into the townsfolk. However many Turks may have been slain, they cannot make up for the defenders who fell with their armour pierced or were dragged down from the walls by Turkish grapnels.

Compared with this attack, all others have been child's play. Last night the sultan was in earnest and a considerable part of his army took part.

When Longo saw the state I was in he gave me friendly counsel: 'In the heat and excitement of battle it's not unusual for a man to put forth strength far exceeding his normal capacity. But nothing is so dangerous as to slacken off during a lull in the fighting, for one is apt to sink down in exhaustion. After that one can hardly struggle to one's knees. For this reason an experienced fighter never exerts all his powers, even in the hottest fray, but keeps something in reserve. It may be the saving of his life if fighting starts again.' He regarded me merrily and added, 'He can at least run away.'

He was in a good humour and was not put out by having to dilute his wine with water as an example to his men. The wine is almost exhausted.

On 16 May Angelos writes:

I could not sleep, therefore, though my position would have permitted me the luxury. Solitude and sleep are the two greatest boons in war. The stars were still twinkling like fine silver needles when I came out, driven by my own restlessness. The night was still and icy cold during these last hours before daybreak.

Near the Kaligari Gate I stopped and listened. It was not only the beating of my heart. I seemed to hear a muffled thudding far beneath my feet. Then I saw Grant the German advancing with a torch in his hand. Tubs of water were ranged behind the wall and he was going from one to another, pausing at each. At first I thought he was out of his mind, or practising exorcism, for it was some way from the wall, and no fire threatened us here.

He greeted me in the name of Christ, shone the light of his flare on the water in one of the tubs and bade me look. At short intervals the dark surface was ruffled by swift, tremulous rings, though the night was still and the guns silent. I said, 'The ground is trembling. Does even the soil of the city quake in mortal terror?' Grant laughed, though his face was sombre.

'Don't you understand what your eyes tell you?' he said. 'If you knew what this meant, cold sweat would break out on the back of your neck as it did on mine just now. Help me to move the tubs, for my assistants have wearied and lain down to sleep.'

Near Between us we shifted the tub a few paces to one side, and Grant thrust a stick into the ground to mark where it had stood. When we had moved it a few more times the surface of the water was again ruffled. I was seized by a superstitious dread as if I were witnessing some black art. Grant, if anyone, should know such mysteries; his face betrays it. He pointed to the winding line of sticks that he had planted in the ground. 'The soil is rocky,' he said. 'As you see, they're having to twist and turn like moles. It will be exciting to watch how far they get before they dare break to the surface.'

'They?' I said, mystified.

'The Turks,' he said. 'They're working under our feet. Didn't you understand?'

'How cunning they are!' I cried. 'They must have begun digging under cover of that nearest mound, more than five hundred paces away. And this is the best place they could have chosen. They have already passed the great wall. What are we to do?'

'Wait,' said Grant calmly. 'There's no danger now that I know how their tunnel runs. It's still far below us. Time enough to act when they turn upwards.' He looked at me grimly. 'I've dug mines myself. It's a terrible task. Never enough air, and constant fear. Death in a mole-run, by fire or water, is a ghastly death indeed.'

Leaving his tubs, he took me with him on a walk along the wall. He had put drums in a number of vaults, with peas on the parchment, but the place where I had seen the water quivering was the only one where he had noticed anything.

'A tunnel is only dangerous if discovered too late,' he explained. 'Luckily, the Turks have attempted to penetrate the city itself. If they had been content to undermine an area under the wall only, propped it with timbers and then set fire to the props, they might have succeeded in bringing down a big stretch of it. But no doubt the ground is unsuitable.'

As the stars paled he told me how to lay a countermine furnished with a movable grille, and how fumes of burning sulphur: are introduced into the enemy saps. 'There are many methods,' he said. 'We can let in water from a cistern and drown them like rats. A flooded tunnel is useless. An even better way is to roast them with Greek fire, for this sets their props alight at the same time and the tunnel falls in. But the most exciting thing is to dig one's own tunnel and lie in wait behind a thin wall to snatch away the diggers. By torturing them one can discover whether other mines have been dug, and if so where.'

His cold-blooded words shocked me. I thought of the men beneath our feet, panting, sweating, blinded by falling earth, toiling like beasts of burden and never guessing that every stroke of the pick brought them nearer a pitiless death.

The next day, shortly after dusk, Grant was summoned to the Kaligari Gate, where this time the Muslims seemed to be working close under the great wall. Here he had already countermined, and his tunnel was now put into use, so that the Muslims suddenly found themselves trapped and were suffocated by poisonous sulphur fumes. Only a couple of men escaped. Grant pierced holes for draught at suitable places, and soon the props in the Muslim mine were one thunderous sea of flame, until the whole passage fell in. But it lay too deep to affect the wall above. Five hundred paces away, black stifling smoke belched up for a long time before the Muslims could block the opening.

When the defenders awoke the next morning, they saw a monstrous marvel looming in front of the wall near the Romanus Gate. In the night, the Muslims had built, with incredible speed and seemingly by the aid of evil spirits, a gigantic travelling wooden siege-tower. It stood on the brink of the moat, only thirty paces from the remains of the outer wall on which the defenders had been toiling all night. Nobody knew how it was done.

This tower, which could be moved by means of huge wooden rollers, was three stories high and overtopped the outer wall. The timbers were everywhere protected from fire by many thicknesses of camel- and ox-hide. The walls were double and packed with earth, so that the defenders' small cannon could not harm them. Arrows whined from the loopholes, and from the topmost platform a mighty mangonel hurled massive blocks of stone to demolish the defenders' temporary earthworks. From the Muslim camp a covered way 500 yards long led into the tower, enabling its crew to come and go freely.

While the mangonel hurled its rocks, while arrows flew and small ballistae slung fire-pots at the palisade and gabions of the outer wall, a row of ports on the bottom storey opened and shut, discharging earth, stones, fascines and timbers into the moat.

When the defenders had gathered horror stricken to behold this tower that worked with no one being visible, a huge shutter in front of the middle platform opened with a great rumbling and a drawbridge shot out towards the outer wall. Luckily, it was too far away for it to reach them. Angelos writes:

> Even Grant hastened up to survey this engine, whose like has never been seen. He measured its dimensions with his eye, noted them down and remarked, 'Although the tower must have been constructed beforehand, and put together by sections on the spot, the mere erecting of it in one night is a marvel of skill and organisation. In itself the tower is no novelty; siege-towers have been used as long as walls. It's only the size which is remarkable. It exceeds any measurements noted by the Greeks and Romans. Were it not for the moat the Turks could wheel it right up to the wall and use it as a ram.'

Having gazed at the tower for a time, he turned and went, for he saw nothing new about its pattern. But Longo ground his teeth and shook his head. It touched his honour that the tower should have been erected unobserved opposite his section of the wall. He said, 'Let us wait until to-night. What man can build he can also destroy.'

But this fort that spews fire, arrows, cannon-balls and stones, and thunders with its own might is so formidable that no one believes Longo. The emperor is at his wits' end; he wept to see many Greek workmen stretched lifeless between the walls by the flying boulders. As long as our outer wall is dominated by this engine, repairs are out of the question. In the afternoon one of the big enemy guns succeeded in shooting away one of the towers on the great wall almost opposite the siege-engine; part of the wall itself collapsed, burying beneath it a number of Latins and Greeks.

That night Angelos helps to burn down the siege-tower. 'In the opinion of many,' he writes the next day, 'this was a greater marvel than the erection of it in a single night. During the darkest hours I lay at its foot. I heard their password. Someone trod on me in the darkness but as I never moved a muscle he took me for a corpse. Two hours before daybreak we forced our way into the tower, smashed open the ports and succeeded in throwing in a few earthenware pots filled with gunpowder. Without these we could never have set it alight. My hair and eyebrows have been singed away and my hands are covered with blisters. Longo did not recognise me when I came crawling back. Of those who entered the tower I am the only survivor. Some of the Turkish occupants escaped. This morning the sultan had them executed and impaled their heads on stakes.'

The following night the Muslims brought up more siege-towers, though none of them as big and menacing as the one Angelos had helped to burn.

On the morning of 22 May two mine tunnels were discovered. One was demolished only after savage fighting. The other fell in of itself, having been unskilfully shored up. Angelos writes that Grant believed most of the expert miners had perished, forcing the Muslims to employ unskilled men.

Constantine's ministers implored him to leave while it was still possible, to head a Byzantine government in exile until able to recover the city. Even as they spoke he fainted from exhaustion. But on recovery he was as resolved as before to remain.

On 26 May Mehmed declared at a council of war that the siege had gone on long enough, that the time had come for the final assault. The next day would be spent on preparations, the day after that to rest and prayer. The assault would commence in the early hours of the morning of the following day.

No attempt was made to hide the plan from the defenders, and it was easy for them to guess that he had fixed the day and the hour for the decisive attack. From the battlements they saw the Muslim commanders assembling by his tent. The war council lasted all afternoon, then messengers galloped off to all parts of the camp to make known his commands. The roars and yells that arose, the jubilant clang and clamour of music and voices surpassed all the defenders had yet heard, and in the evening increased to a constant thunder.

For the next thirty-six hours the preparatory work continued incessantly. Soldiers whetted their blades and cut up cloth to make pennants of with their lances, so that each man could mark out his claim to a house and everything and everyone in it. Anyone who could write inscribed his pennant with a Muslim slogan or a verse from the *Koran*, the favourite being 61:13, 'And He will bestow upon you other blessings that you desire: help from Allah and a speedy victory. Proclaim the good tidings to the faithful'. At night huge flares were lit to help the soldiers at their labours, while drums and trumpets encouraged them, Then, at dawn on the 28th, all was suddenly silent. Mehmed went on a long tour of inspection, returning to his tent at dusk.

As the Muslims had made no attempt to conceal their plan, Angelos observes and hears everything. His journal entry for 28 May reads, 'Today the enemy have been preparing their assault, and through the darkness can be heard a low, unbroken murmur as they bring forward their scaling-ladders, beams, bridges and fascines. Their fires were lit only for a short time, and were extinguished when the sultan allowed his men a few hours' rest before the attack.'

The assault began at 1.30 a.m. with a cataclysmic bombardment unprecedented in the long history of siege warfare. The stone missiles from all the Muslims' heavy guns, including the giant cannon, smashed the city's breastworks. The din of falling timber filled the air. The walls were pulverised. Defenders manning them struggled to suppress urges of violent trembling and lost control of bodily functions. Some were buried alive when the section of the wall they were cowering behind collapsed.

Orban too was killed, along with an entire gun crew, when one of his cannon exploded, 'hoisted by his own petard'. This archaic saying, coined by Shakespeare in *Hamlet*, means to be blown up by your own gun or bomb, to have a plan backfire on you. A petard was a primitive bomb, and a petardier a dangerous occupation. The fuses were unreliable and often exploded prematurely. Cannon, too, were apt to go off before plan.

And then, the walls destroyed, before the dust had settled and the smoke dispersed, with the sudden clamour of blasts of trumpets, beating of drums and tens of thousands of troops screaming *'Allahu akbar!'*, the poorly armed and untrained *bashi-bazouks* hurled themselves against the ruins. Church bells pealed, signalling to the whole city that the final infantry assault had started.

After two hours the few surviving *bashi-bazouks* withdrew, their attack ebbing as the first light of dawn appeared in the sky. The defenders' bodies were tender and bruised all over, and their arms were so weary that after each stroke they fancied that they could not raise them for another. But, at the withdrawal, hope revived in some and a poor fool here and there could be heard shouting, 'Victory!' The experienced Genoese, however, panting and wheezing in their iron armour and gasping for water, knew that the torment was not over.

And indeed, the expendable irregulars were immediately replaced by several regiments of superbly trained and disciplined Anatolian Turks.

Angelos writes, 'These were swift, savage men who laughed gleefully as they clambered up on each other's shoulders in swarms to reach the top of the rampart. They had no need to be whipped forward, for they were true Turks with war in their blood. They asked no quarter and died with the name of Allah on their lips. They knew that the ten thousand angels of Islam were hovering overhead and at the moment of death would snatch each one of them straight up to paradise. They attacked in close waves of a thousand, yelling and reviling the Christians with menaces too frightful to record. But our men stood their ground. The gaps in our ranks were filled, and wherever the living wall of iron seemed to waver there dashed Longo, to encourage his men and cleave Turks to the midriff with his two-handed sword. Wherever he appeared, there the assault slackened and the enemy raised their ladders at some other point.'

And then it was the turn of the best infantry of all – the élite janissaries.

'One could now distinguish a black thread from a white, and as night faded we could make out the tall white felt caps of the janissaries in well-dressed ranks opposite, on the other side of the ditch,' writes Angelos. 'They stood in companies of a thousand, one behind the other, silently awaiting the order to attack. Sultan Mehmed himself could be glimpsed in front of them, bearing his iron hammer of command. Hastily we trained culverins and arquebuses on him and fired, but failed to hit him. Several janissaries fell round about him, but the ranks stood motionless. Fresh men stepped forward to fill the gaps, and I knew that they rejoiced in the honour of joining the front rank beneath the eye of their sultan, a position to which neither their age nor length of service would otherwise have entitled them. Green-clad men quickly placed themselves between us and the sultan, to shield him with their own bodies.

'The women and old men on the great wall took advantage of this pause to lower big jars of water mixed with wine; for although even this main rampart was so badly damaged that at many points it stood no higher than the earthwork before it, it was still too steep to climb down.

'What followed I can merely relate as I saw it, and perhaps another would tell the story differently, since man's powers of observation are always faulty. Nevertheless, I was standing close by Longo outside the sally-port and I believe I saw what happened.

'A glowing discus sped across the sky. I heard the warning shouts in time and threw myself down as the Turks once more discharged their great cannon and all their other pieces in a tremendous volley. The wind had freshened and soon swept away the rolling black clouds of smoke.

As the din and the cries died away I saw Longo slowly sink down and sit upon the ground. At one side of his cuirass gaped a hole the size of my fist, from a leaden ball that had struck him diagonally from the rear. In an instant his face turned grey and all vitality drained from him, so that he seemed an old man, despite his freshly-dyed hair and beard. He spat out a mouthful of blood, and blood was also running down the fold of his groin below the armour. He said, "This is the end of me."

'The men nearest to him shouted for a surgeon but the Greeks on the wall replied that no one could get to him, since the postern was locked. A brave man might have slid down the face of the wall but it was understandable that no physician was willing to do this even for Longo's sake, for just then the copper drums of the janissaries began to roll and they struck up their assault-music. It is beneath the janissaries' dignity to invoke Allah as they charge. They raced silently, savagely towards our earthwork. In many places they had no need of ladders, so high lay the heaps of corpses before the ruins of our outer wall. Their onslaught was swift and violent, and few of the defenders had time to drink, though we were all perishing with thirst. Jars of water were knocked over beside us and in another moment a hand-to-hand struggle was raging all along the top of the wall.

'The janissaries wore either scale-armour or chain-mail. Their swords struck swiftly as lightning and by sheer weight of numbers they forced the defenders back. The Genoese and the Greeks who had been sent to our relief were compelled to bunch up in order to resist the pressure with united strength.

'Just then the emperor, mounted on his white charger, showed himself upon the battlements. His face glowed and he shouted jubilantly, "Stand fast! Stand fast but once more, and the day is ours!" Had he been down there among us and felt the leaden weight of our limbs he would have held his peace.

'Longo raised his bull's head from his hands, gritted his teeth in agony, spat out another blood-clot and with a coarse oath bade the emperor hand over the key of the sally-port. The emperor shouted in reply that his wound could not be as serious as all that, and that it would be unbecoming in him to forsake his men just now on account of his present pain. Longo shrieked in reply, "I'm the best judge of that! Throw down that key or I'll come up and strangle you with my own hands!"

'Even in the fury of battle his men burst out laughing, and after a moment's hesitation the emperor threw down the great key at Longo's very feet. He picked it up and showed it meaningly to those nearest him. The conflict was raging only a few paces away, loud with the clash and squeal of blades on armour. There a huge janissary was laying about him with a captured two-handed sword, until the iron-clad Genoese contrived to surround him and bring him to his knees. So impregnable was his armour that they had to slay him piecemeal.

'As the first wave of janissaries withdrew to get their breath the next surged forward. Longo called to me and said, "Give me your arm and help me away from here. A good commander fights so long as there's a chance, but no longer."

'I took one arm and the man nearest him the other, and we succeeded in getting him down the rampart and through the sally-port into the city. The emperor met us in great agitation, attended by his suite. He was without armour, so as to move more freely, and wore a purple shirt and a mantle of imperial green stitched with gold. Once more he urged Longo to stand fast and return to the battle; the wound, he said, was not necessarily so serious. But Longo never answered, nor even looked at him; he had enough to do to endure the hideous agony that every step entailed.

'The emperor returned to the wall to observe the course of the battle and encourage the Greeks with his counsel. We managed to remove Longo's armour; blood slopped from it as it fell to the ground. He signed to his next in command and said, "You will answer for the men's lives." The officer nodded and returned to the wall.

'Longo's few surviving Genoese helped him on to the back of his great charger to take him to the harbour and with drawn swords surrounded him in a threatening group to prevent others seeing that he was wounded. I waved to him and shouted, "Good luck! May you soon be well again!" But from his leaden face and closed eyes I saw that it was a dying man the soldiers were leading to the harbour. He could no longer turn his head to answer. His men supported him in the saddle on both sides.'

The janissaries advanced at the double in wave after wave across the plain, kept in step by deafening military music and kettle drums, huge drums thumped by four men simultaneously on a horse cart.

The fighting lasted six hours, during which time the defenders had no rest. With the janissaries now pouring through the open breaches, the ultimate fate of the exhausted last Byzantine emperor, named Constantine like the first, is unknown. Some say he ran to where the fighting was thickest and was slain alongside his soldiers. According to one story, Muslim soldiers recognised the body by the imperial double-headed eagles embroidered on his purple boots, and a janissary was later seen carrying such an ornate pair of boots but would not reveal where he got them and all his colleagues had themselves so much plunder no one felt inclined to pursue the matter. One report says a janissary cut the emperor's head from his corpse lying among the other bodies and took it to the sultan, saying, 'There you have the head of your cruellest foe.' But Barbaro wrote in his journal that the emperor hanged himself at the moment the janissaries broke in at the Romanus Gate.

In the evening Muslim troops began gathering from all parts, and along the main street Mehmed's brilliant retinue advanced, escorted by runners swinging censers. The horses trod on corpses of Christians still lying in the street, and curly-haired young eunuchs of the *harem* sprinkled rose-water in front of the sultan's white charger. Mehmed, his fiery lean young face twitching with weariness, dismounted at the bronze gates of St Sophia, the Great Church of Holy Wisdom, which had been forced, and with his entourage entered the cathedral, in which thousands of citizens were hiding, not understanding that Muslims would not observe the sacred law of sanctuary. The citizens were all either being slain or being taken as slaves. Pretty females were being raped, soldiers fighting each other to the death over the most beautiful. Symbols of Christianity were being vandalised or destroyed, though the crucifix was saved in order to be later paraded through the Muslims' camps.

Mehmed admired the flagstones, made of local Proconnesian marble, white with rippling bands of grey, resembling a frozen sea. On this lovely floor lay bloodstained corpses, and one corner of it was already submerged under the prayer mats of janissaries, a crowd of whom were busy looting, tearing away the gold and silver frames of icons and collecting all valuables in altar cloths and pearl-embroidered vestments. Mehmed halted a soldier hacking at the valuable marble floor. Looting, he said, did not extend to the destruction of public buildings, for they all now belonged to him. 'Be satisfied with the booty and captives,' he said.

Meanwhile, Angelos is writing the last page of his journal:

To write this fittingly I should dip my pen in blood. And blood would not be lacking. Blood fills the gutters in a congealed and sticky sludge. Blood from the wounds of the dying collects in warm pools. In the main street by the Hippodrome and about the great church lie so many corpses that one can hardly walk there without treading upon them.

I have stuffed my ears with wax to escape the shrieks of outraged women and children, the howls of pillagers lighting over their spoils, the ceaseless death-cry rising from my city.

I am forcing myself into detachment. I write, although my hand shakes. I am shaking all over not from fear, not on my own account; my life is worth less than a grain of sand in the street, but on account of the suffering and pain now welling from a thousand sources round me on this day of boundless terror.

I have seen a young girl, marked by bloody hands, throw herself down a well. I have seen a wretch tear a babe from its mother and laughingly impale it on a comrade's spear, so as to be free to throw down the woman. I have seen all the worst that human beings can do to one another.

I met the German, Johann Grant, and dismounted from my horse to embrace him and thank him for his friendship. His face was peppered with gunpowder, he moved painfully and blinked his smarting eyes continually. But even on this last evening he was entirely given over to his insatiable desire for knowledge. He pointed to two aged, bald and toothless men who were staggering by, led by a youth in the costume of an imperial technician on which was a red badge of honour which I had not seen before.

'Do you know who those are?' he asked. I shook my head and he told me, 'They come from the most secret underground chamber in the arsenal where Greek fire is made. Do you see how yellow the boy's face is, and how thin his hair? The old men have lost all their teeth and their skin is peeling. I should much like to talk to them, but they're guarded, and anyone seeking to address them is cut down on the spot.

'Their stock of raw materials is exhausted,' he went on. 'The last remaining crocks of fluid have now been carried to the wall and to the ships. I know some of the ingredients, but not all, nor how they are blended. The most remarkable feature is the way the fluid ignites of itself as soon as it spurts out. It's not the effect of the air, but of some combustible in the vessels themselves; there must be some device in the muzzle of the mortar that sets it burning. There's a good deal of naphtha in it, since it floats on water, and water cannot put it out. Only sand and vinegar can quench it. The Venetian sailors say that at a pinch they can extinguish stray drops of it with urine. Those old fellows are the last who know the secret, which has been preserved for a thousand years.

'No one has ever been allowed to write it down, and in former days they cut out the tongues of all who worked in the underground chambers. The last duty of the arsenal guards will be to kill these old men, so that they may carry their secret to the grave. That's why they have been allowed to come to church today for the first time for who knows how many years.'

He shrugged his shoulders. 'Many secrets will perish with this city, much priceless knowledge. And to no purpose. John Angelos, there is nothing more detestable than war. I say this, after having destroyed many Turkish mine-tunnels and used all my skill and art in helping the emperor's technicians to kill more Turks than ever before.'

All the way to the Valens aqueduct the main street was strewn with the corpses of slain Christians. There the slaughtering had ended. Long strings of citizens were bound together, casually guarded only by one or two of the few *bashi-bazouks* who had survived the initial Muslim suicide attack. The women had been robbed of their jewels, their clothes were torn from being searched for hidden money, and their hands were tied behind them with their own girdles. Elderly people and children, artisans and the wealthy, walked side by side, to be separated later in the Muslim camp, that the poor might be sold as slaves and the rich pay their ransoms. A throng of fat, rich Genoese traders gathered in the city to buy plunder to sell at great profit in Pera. Many of the Muslim wounded who should have survived, having received good medical attention, died because their comrades withheld sustenance, leaving more booty for themselves.

From most of the houses fluttered the personal pennant of the victor who had claimed that house for his own. From within these houses could be heard the weeping and screaming of many women and girls.

Females had been the initial lure. Immediately the city fell, the conquering soldiers and sailors had raced each other to be among the first to reach the wives, sisters and daughters of the slain defenders whose body parts littered the shattered walls. Heads, torsos and limbs were strewn around, the ground slippery with blood, gore, intestines, brains and bone marrow. Barbaro wrote that the slaughter continued throughout the day, describing blood flowing in the city 'like rainwater in the gutters after a sudden storm' and bodies of Christians floating in the sea 'like melons along a canal'. In the Golden Horn harbour the air was thick with bad odours, putrid and sickly. Corpses bobbed in a suppurating froth of yellow and pink water. Between them floated body parts: a purple and shiny leg, a torso in sodden clothes, a hand like a glove, with nothing beyond the wrist... The corpses and bits of people gave off a fleshy and sweet stench of sulphated oxygen.

Normally, victorious Muslim forces were granted three days to rape and plunder but on this occasion all the loot had gone by dusk and the next day was devoted to barter as it was exchanged or sold. Traumatised women and girls were passed around, either thrown in as a makeweight to clinch a deal or sold as sex slaves. Following the slaying of their menfolk they were now being serially raped by successive men, the city resonating with their wailing and screams. In St Sophia, the senior *imam* mounted the pulpit and intoned the proclamation that prefixes all but one of the *Koran*'s chapters: 'In the Name of Allah, the Compassionate, the Merciful.'

Chapter 4

Suleiman I and the Battle of Mohács

After the capture of Constantinople, the Ottomans continued with the familiar Muslim policy of expansion through military conquest. Mehmed was now called *El Fati*, 'the Conqueror', and his armies swept almost from one victory to another, advancing westwards at an alarming rate, despite setbacks. He rallied his resources in order to subjugate the kingdom of Hungary, his immediate objective being the border fortress town of Belgrade. Situated on a promontory at the confluence of the Danube with its tributary the Sava, the Serbian town was the key fortress of the defence of the kingdom's southern frontier. The Ottomans had failed to conquer it in a siege sixteen years earlier.

This time, after envoys from Croatia had warned the Hungarian leaders that the Muslims were preparing to invade Hungary again, with a force of more than 100,000 men, and few barons had heeded the command to send levies for a national call up, a Franciscan friar named John of Capistrano preached fiery sermons for an anti-Muslim crusade. His oratory roused 60,000 local peasants, who assembled at the fortress in early July. They were augmented by 5,000 Hungarian, Czech and Polish mercenaries hired by the Hungarian general, John Hunyadi, who also assembled a flotilla of 200 ships on the Danube that destroyed the Muslim fleet, preventing the Muslims from completing the blockade, which enabled Hunyadi and his relief force to enter the fortress and reinforce the defence.

The life of Hunyadi (pronounced 'Hoonyadi') had been one unbroken struggle against the constantly invading Muslims. In command of the defence of the southern frontier, he had mastered his military skills on the borderlands that were exposed to the Muslim attacks and, though he lost two battles, he was successful in his long two-year campaign across the Balkan mountains and already had a reputation as a great general when the siege began with an artillery bombardment of the walls followed up seventeen days later by infantry assaults.

The siege escalated into a major battle when a sudden spontaneous, unauthorised sortie by the fort's motley army of crusader peasants overran the Ottoman camp, compelling Mehmed, who had been wounded by an arrow in the thigh, to retreat.

Hunyadi died three weeks later in a plague epidemic that broke out among the defenders.

The peasant crusaders' victory over the sultan who had conquered Constantinople was hailed throughout Europe. Processions celebrating the triumph were made in Venice and Oxford. Hunyadi's fame was a decisive factor in the election of his son, Matthias Corvinus, as Hungarian king the following year, and Hunyadi is a major folk hero in Hungary, Romania, Serbia, Bulgaria and other countries of the region. During the siege, the pope had ordered that Christian churches ring their bells at noon to gather the faithful in prayer for those who were fighting, and noon bells in support of the war against invading Muslims have remained a widespread church tradition in eastern Europe and the Balkans to this day.

Undeterred, Mehmed continued his conquests, massacring the entire Croatian armed forces and invading what is now Romania – where he met strong resistance from a bloodthirsty prince named Draculea.

In the year Draculea was born his father had been vested into the Order of the Dragon, a fellowship of knights sworn to defend Christendom against the encroaching Muslims. During the initiation in Nuremberg his father was given the epithet Dracul, *dragon*, so his son had the patronymic of Draculea, the inspiration for the name of the vampire in Bram Stoker's 1897 gothic novel.

The son became known as Vlad Țepeș (pronounced Tsepesh), 'Vlad the Impaler', after his favourite means of execution. To the Muslims he was known as *Kazikli Bey* (Impaler Lord) when their armies had seen his 'forests' of impalement victims. One such forest had 20,000 corpses. Another was of 1,000 Muslim cavalrymen whom Draculea had ambushed. Their leader was impaled on the tallest stake to show his high rank.

Draculea's father had reluctantly agreed to pay the tribute demanded of him by the Ottomans, despite his affiliation with the Order of the Dragon, and Draculea and his brother Radu ('the Handsome') were taken into Ottoman custody as hostages. During his childhood and adolescence spent in Ottoman captivity, Draculea learned of the method of impalement as an execution and to speak fluent Turkish.

Released after his father had been assassinated, he returned to his principality of Wallachia (not neighbouring Transylvania, as in *Dracula*) and impaled the noblemen who had conspired in the assassination. He restored order to the destabilised principality, showing no mercy toward criminals, or anyone who plotted against his rule.

He also fiercely resisted Ottoman rule, sometimes repelling the Ottomans and sometimes forced to retreat and compromise. Sultan Mehmed once sent an envoy, a Greek named Thomas Katabolinos, to Wallachia to summon Draculea to Constantinople, at the same time as sending an instruction to Hamza, bey of Nicopolis, to seize Draculea after he had crossed the Danube. Draculea discovered the sultan's 'deceit and trickery', captured Hamza and Katabolinos, and had them both impaled.

Draculea twice exhibited extraordinary audacity. After the ambush of the cavalrymen he disguised his troops in their uniforms and, disguised in such a uniform himself, he approached a Turkish-held fortress and called out to the commander in his flawless Turkish that they were survivors of the ambush and needed to be let in. The gates were opened and he led in his troops, who then threw off their disguise and massacred all in the deceived garrison. And he thwarted an offensive by Mehmed with a famed night attack on the invaders' camp that included a plan for him personally to stab the sleeping sultan. This plan failed because Draculea entered the wrong tent and slew the wrong man, but the audacity so frightened Mehmed that he abandoned the campaign.

The daring attack was an act of desperation, as Draculea had been forced to retreat and to accept a demand to pay an increased tribute and could see no choice. He died in battle in 1477 and Mehmed replaced him by his compliant and good-looking brother, Radu the Handsome. Some reports suggest Mehmed was bisexual. He spared young men condemned to death if he found them attractive, adding them to his seraglio, and Radu may have been a favourite.

Mehmed had boasted he would turn the Vatican into a big mosque, the same as he had the cathedral of St Sophia in Constantinople, and in 1480 he launched the campaign that has been called the 'Invasion of Italy'. On 28 July a huge Ottoman fleet landed near the town of Otranto on the heel of Italy, whereupon the garrison and the citizens retreated to its citadel. Two weeks later this fort was taken by the invaders, who massacred the garrison and 10,000 citizens. Thousands more were enslaved. The Muslims rounded up 800 male citizens and herded them into the cathedral, where the archbishop, a bishop and the garrison commander were sawn in two alive. The next day the 800 survivors were beheaded for refusing to convert to Islam. The cathedral was then used as a stable. In September a monastery containing one of the finest libraries of Europe was destroyed, and the following month the Muslim forces attacked the coastal towns of Lecce, Taranto and Brindisi and later conquered the beautiful land of Montenegro, just across the Adriatic from Italy.

Mehmed also tried to conquer Rhodes, island fortress of Christian military order the Knights of St John, only ten miles from the coast of Anatolia, Ottoman territory. The Knights of St John, originally established in Palestine in the eleventh century to tend sick pilgrims, had been evicted with the last of the Crusaders from the Holy Land in 1291. After a long search for a suitable new base, followed by a three-year siege, in 1310 they had captured Rhodes, a province of Byzantium, which they had made their headquarters and which, by a papal decree, became their property. In these circumstances they were not just an order of knighthood but also a sovereign state. On arrival they had immediately built their new infirmary, which soon became the most celebrated, and by far the best, hospital in the world. Its great ward could hold eight-five patients, all tended by the knights themselves.

Mehmed sent an army of 70,000 against them, carried in a fleet of fifty ships. Also on board were several of the formidable cannon that had smashed the walls of Constantinople. Against this huge host the knights disposed 600 members of their order, together with 1,500 foreign mercenaries and local militia. After the first three weeks of the siege the walls began to crumble and the knights' leader was seriously wounded, but somehow the defenders held firm. Then, suddenly, panic spread through the Muslim lines; the *bashi-bazouks* turned and fled, the rest of the army behind them. No one knows why this happened but, whatever the reason, the Muslims' triumph was transformed from one moment to the next into disaster. Mehmed immediately began preparing a fresh army, but in the spring of 1481, as he was riding through Asia Minor he suffered a fatal heart attack, aged only 49. Mehmed, like his father, was also obese, and he too died young of over-eating.

His sons Bayezid and Djem raced to the Ottoman capital to capture the throne. Bayezid got there first and was declared Sultan Bayezid the Second. As the death of an Ottoman monarch usually provoked clashes for supremacy resembling the mating season of amorous male beasts, princes strutting or skulking depending on the outcome, flaunting their triumph or licking their wounds, Djem, in mortal danger, desperately fled to the victorious Christian knights on Rhodes. The Ottomans had no law of primogeniture. Instead they had the law of the jungle. In this anarchic system of succession of the fittest, sometimes the power struggle was clean and swift, other times a messy prolonged civil war.

In 1512 Bayezid II's son Selim ('the Grim') became the Ottoman sultan, with the usual ferocity. His brother Ahmed was the legal heir to the throne but, when Bayezid officially announced Ahmed as heir apparent, Selim rebelled and while he lost the first battle against his father's forces, only escaping with 3,000 men out of 30,000, he ultimately deposed his father, exiling him to the north-east of present-day Greece, where Bayezid died immediately, apparently poisoned by Selim, who then also had Ahmed strangled by bowstring, as well as another brother and five orphan nephews. A son of Ahmed fled to the neighbouring Persian empire of Shah Ismail of the Safavid dynasty, who had supported his father.

The Safavids were of the Shi'ite sect, while the Ottomans were of the rival Sunni sect, and early in his reign Selim instructed his officials to undertake a census of people thought to be Safavid sympathisers in east Anatolian cities and, as he marched through these cities, his forces rounded up and beheaded all those registered who could be found,

40,000 of them; and then, after he had exchanged a series of belligerent letters with Ismail, in 1514 he attacked Ismail's kingdom, partly because Ismail had supported Ahmed but also to halt the growing influence of the Safavids in Ottoman dominions.

Selim defeated Ismail at the Battle of Chaldiran because the Ottomans, who had been early masters of gunpowder warfare, had more than a hundred large-calibre modern cannon, while the shah's army was entirely cavalry – the cannon's tremendous roar terrified the Persian horses, who turned and stampeded. In their terror they ignored their riders' bits or spurs and scattered and divided themselves over the plain. Ismail was wounded and almost captured and Selim triumphally entered the Safavid capital of Tabriz unopposed, his troops looting the imperial treasury and pillaging the town before evacuating. The defeat traumatised Ismail. He became an alcoholic and withdrew from state affairs, leaving them to a vizier who was a close friend and drinking companion before being assassinated a few years later.

Selim captured Ismail's *harem* and two of his wives, one of whom was Ismail's favourite. Selim married her to an Ottoman *kadi*, or judge. Ismail sent four envoys, gifts and, in contrast to their previous exchanges, words of praise to Selim, in order to help retrieve her. Instead of giving him back his favourite missus, however, Selim cut off the envoys' noses.

Selim then invaded and conquered the Mamluke sultanate of Egypt even though the Mamluke state religion was Sunni. He extinguished the Mamluke dynasty, hanging its last sultan.

Selim's conquest of the Middle Eastern heartlands of the Muslim world established the Ottoman empire as the most prestigious of all Muslim states. Short-tempered, he was severe with subordinates; he executed several of his viziers for various reasons, hence his epithet of 'the Grim'. Because of his successful campaigns and victorious battles he was also called 'Allah's Shadow' and has a whole Muslim hagiographic genre devoted to him, the 'tales of Selim'. He spent every campaigning season of his adult life astride a saddle, and died of an anthrax skin infection. Anthrax was an occupational hazard among saddlers, tanners, skinners and others who worked with leather. He was interred in a shrine mosque specially built by his son and successor, Suleiman.

When Suleiman became sultan at the age of 25, he was already an experienced ruler. Ten years earlier he had been appointed governor of Caffa, which the Ottomans had captured from the waning Mongols, where he remained for three years; subsequently Selim appointed him governor of Constantinople. In that decade Selim had instituted his reign of terror, seeming to conceive of government solely in terms of executions, so that, by the time of his succession, Suleiman was the only male member of his entire family left alive.

Nor were Selim's executions by any means confined to his family. He had thought nothing, for example, of condemning to death 400 Turkish merchants who had disobeyed his edict by trading with Persia. Therefore it was not surprising that his son's accession was everywhere greeted as a new dawn. And so it was: unjustly held captives were released, trade with Persia re-established, corrupt or sadistic officials brought to justice and hanged.

Still he made it clear that though his reign was to be just it would also be uncompromisingly firm, writing to the governor of Egypt, 'My sublime commandment, as inescapable as and as binding as fate, is that rich and poor, town and country, subjects and payers of tribute – everybody must hasten to obey. If some of them are slow to do their duty, do not hesitate to inflict on them the ultimate punishment.'

He also made it clear that he was not averse to assuming the title of ruler of the world. His warlike predecessors had annihilated the Serbian, Bulgarian and Byzantine empires. That left the kingdom of Hungary as the closest land still to be conquered. Hungary had played a stalwart part in the resistance against the Muslims, but after the death of Corvinus in 1490 it had notably declined in power and prestige, which its present king, Louis the Second, seemed unlikely to regain.

Muslims had always yearned to conquer Europe, and Suleiman knew that Hungary was the key. And, as well as internal chaos limiting the Hungarians' ability to defend themselves, the political climate in the rest of Europe ensured they would receive little or no aid against a Muslim invasion. Europe was a divided continent whose great powers were locked in perpetual feuds. France, the Polish-Lithuanian Union and the Holy Roman Empire dominated by the Habsburg dynasty all had their own agendas that precluded co-operation. These states were too pre-occupied in a struggle over control of Italy to pay any attention to the belligerent Muslim empire at their doorstep. Suleiman intended to exploit this.

So, under him, the Ottomans again invaded Hungary, again starting with Belgrade, the mighty fortress standing at the confluence of the Sava river and the Danube, the effective gateway to Hungary and the Danube valley through which he could take his armies straight to Buda and Vienna. In 1456 Hunyadi had successfully defended it against his great-grandfather Mehmed II, who had been seriously wounded in the assault, a setback that Suleiman was determined to avenge. Three weeks of heavy bombardment were followed by a successful assault after the Muslim sappers blew up the fortress's main tower. Muslims occupied the garrison town and it became a vital military base for further Muslim campaigns in Hungary. Belgrade soon had a population exceeding 100,000, making it the second biggest town in the Ottoman empire, surpassed only by the capital, Constantinople.

When the news reached western Europe that one of the greatest Christian strongholds of the east had fallen to Islam, its biggest church converted into a mosque, there was general consternation. It was feared the Muslims would immediately march on Buda and after that press on along the Danube to Vienna. But Suleiman turned his attention to another Christian foe, the Knights of St John on Rhodes.

The Rhodes fortress, following its pounding by Mehmed's giant cannon in 1480, had been rebuilt at great expense according to designs by leading Italian engineers. It was divided into bastions according to the nationality of the knights defending that segment, huge, angled towers that would permit covering fire along exposed sections of the walls and strengthening the ramparts.

Within a fortnight of assuming office in 1521 the knights' Grand Master, Philippe Villiers de l'Isle Adam, a deeply pious French aristocrat aged 57 who had spent most of his life on the island, had received a letter from Suleiman in which the sultan boasted of the conquests he had already made, including those of Belgrade and 'many other fine and well-fortified cities, of which I killed most of the inhabitants and reduced the rest to slavery'. Its implications were obvious but de l'Isle Adam refused to be intimidated. In his reply he proudly reported his own recent victory over a notorious Turkish pirate named Cortoglu who had tried to capture him. Then, in the early summer of 1522, Suleiman sent another missive to the knights of Rhodes: 'The monstrous injuries that you have inflicted upon my most long-suffering people have aroused my pity and my wrath. I command you therefore instantly to surrender the island and fortress of Rhodes, and I give you my gracious permission to depart in safety with your most valued possessions. If you are wise you will prefer friendship and peace to the cruelties of war.' Suleiman added that any knights who wished to remain could do so, provided only that they acknowledged his sovereignty. De l'Isle Adam ignored this letter.

The first ships of the 700-strong Muslim fleet from Gallipoli appeared in the northern horizon on 26 June. Over the next two days more vessels joined this vanguard, including the flagship carrying the sultan himself. The force was so big it took a month to disembark.

Only 703 knights defended the whole fortress, along with 6,000 locals determined to protect their homes and families; contingents from the various commanderies of the order throughout Europe; 500 Cretan archers; and 1,500 other mercenaries. Despite the defenders being massively outnumbered, the defences were so strong as to be thought by many to be impregnable; and all the wheat on the island had been harvested and stored, which, as well as providing ample food for the siege, had the bonus of denying the Muslims the possibility of living off the land.

On arrival, Suleiman made himself comfortable in a ceremonial red tent out of the range of cannon fire.

The defenders had to maintain a constant vigil over every bit of the wall, repairing damage as soon as it was inflicted and watching for any sign among the Muslims that might suggest the activity of sappers. Mining had become a speciality with Ottoman armies, who understood that many impressive fortifications were much more vulnerable from beneath than from the front.

By mid-September the defenders' worst fears were realised when they discovered no fewer than fifty tunnels running in various directions under the wall. Luckily they had secured the services of the greatest military engineer of the time, an Italian named Gabriele Tadini, who had constructed his own warren of tunnels, from which he could listen – with the aid of tightly stretched drums of parchment capable of picking up every blow of a Muslim spade – and often de-activate the enemy fuses. But he could not succeed every time, and two mines detonated beneath the English bastion, collapsing a long segment of the wall. The Muslims poured into the breach and there followed two hours of bitter hand-to-hand fighting before the defenders prevailed. In this exchange both sides took heavy casualties. The sultan's master gunner's legs were blown off by a cannonball, while three major commanders of the knights were slain. The bastion became the most heavily fought over in the siege.

Weeks of constant shelling reduced walls to rubble. Throughout October fighting continued back and forth, mostly around the collapsed wall of the English bastion. By December more than half the knights were either dead or hopelessly wounded, and de l'Isle Adam was reluctantly persuaded by the locals to surrender.

On the morning of Christmas Day a group of janissaries determined to show what fine upright Muslims they were forcibly entered the great St John Church, defaced the frescos, broke up the tombs, scattered the ashes of the dead, dragged the crucifix in the dust, turned the altars upside down and, before departing, slew some Christians who had either resisted their entrance or given them dirty looks at the desecration. The church was then converted into a mosque.

On the evening of New Year's Day de l'Isle Adam and the other Christian survivors, including a future successor, a young Gascon knight named Jean de La Valette, a hard, implacable defender of Christianity, utterly single-minded in the service of the order, sailed for Crete.

With the great Christian fortress of Rhodes taken, Suleiman gained dominance in the Mediterranean and could now direct all his resources once more towards the mainland, again targeting Hungary on the northern border of his empire, a vulnerable kingdom rife with internal chaos. In April 1526 a huge Muslim army with 300 cannon embarked on an eighty-day march up the Balkans, during which torrential rains flooded the rivers, including the Danube, making maintenance of supply lines difficult. When the invaders reached the town of Osijek they had to build a long bridge over the swollen Drava. It was completed in five days and immediately the last soldier had crossed it, it was destroyed, cutting off any means of retreat.

The Hungarian king, Louis, was in a dire situation. He had written to Henry VIII, 'If assistance from Your Majesty does not arrive soon my kingdom is lost.' Henry did not respond.

Louis did, however, slowly gather troops, until his army grew to about 25,000, comprising 12,000 cavalry and 13,000 infantry. Few aristocrats had heeded his call to the colours. After he summoned them to assemble on 2 July, not one turned up. Those who were prepared to fight at all pressed him to engage the enemy at once, without even waiting for the armies of an ambitious aristocrat named John Zápolya, who coveted the throne, or Croatian count Christoph Frankopan – another 35,000 men – which were only a few days' march away.

Louis moved his army south to the plain of Mohács, near a riverside hamlet of that name. Rumours that Suleiman's force numbered 300,000 caused Louis and some of his advisers to waver. He was persuaded to stand firm by the confident arguments of a Roman Catholic monk, Archbishop Pál Tomori, a formidable warrior, who correctly estimated Turkish strength (still vastly superior to the Hungarians') and discounted their capabilities. For some reason Tomori had been given supreme command. His astonishing over-confidence was due to his blind belief in the Hungarian cavalry, of which both horses and riders were so completely encased in armour they were unable to manoeuvre when confronted by lightly-armed enemy counterparts such as the Ottomans' cavalry. Tomori himself glittered in a distinctive suit of golden Renaissance armour. He had forgotten, too – if indeed he had ever understood – the power of the Muslims' artillery with its huge cannon, firing iron cannonballs that exploded on impact.

Suleiman's light reconnaissance cavalry, on reaching the southern edge of the plain, discovered the Hungarian army prepared for battle in the middle of it south-west of the hamlet. He sent a detachment of 6,000 by a circuitous route to the west, taking advantage of undulations of the ground, to launch a surprise attack on the Hungarian right after the armies were fully engaged.

The battle began at 2.00 p.m. in pelting rain. The advancing Muslims were met by a cannonade. The Hungarian heavy cavalry then charged to drive back their first line. Following this initial success, the rest of the Hungarian army advanced but the heavy guns could not keep up. Just as the Hungarian cavalry charged again, the Muslims' hidden enveloping force hit them on the right flank as planned, throwing them into considerable confusion. And then when the Hungarian infantry charged they suffered heavy casualties from the Muslim artillery. Another Hungarian cavalry charge reached the sultan's bodyguard of janissaries, several of whom were slain. He survived when they hamstrung the assailants' horses. Archbishop Tomori fought bravely in his gold armour, which was now dripping wet and oozing blood. An Ottoman historian wrote: 'Like cast iron, the more the battle struck him, the more he steeped himself in it and drew strength from it. Like a viper or an elephant, he held his own against the claws of combat or the stones cast in battle. Covered with wounds, like a mad dog he recovered himself. When he rushed into the attack, impetuous as the Nile, he uttered screams like the trumpeting of elephants when tigers and lions flee before them.'

Tomori died in a Muslim counter-attack at dusk in which, unable or unwilling to follow his example, most of his exhausted compatriots fled, including Louis. In the tumult, Louis's terrified horse threw him into a flooded brook, and his heavy armour dragged him down to the bottom, where he drowned. Fifteen thousand Hungarian soldiers had been slain. Muslim fanfares rang out in honour of the victory until midnight. In the morning the sultan, seated on a golden throne in his ceremonial red tent, received congratulations and distributed rewards. The next day 2,000 prisoners of war were decapitated, Suleiman watching from his throne in torrential rain. The skulls were then piled up to form a victorious pyramid. Among them were those of six bishops and that of Archbishop Tomori.

Suleiman spent three days on the battlefield re-organising his force and waiting to see what the Hungarians would do next, unable to believe their small, suicidal army was all they could muster, then cautiously advanced to the town of Buda, marching in unopposed. He decided not to annex Hungary. He made it a tributary kingdom under Zápolya. The victorious Muslims then returned home, taking with them the spoils of war, as usual.

Civil war engulfed Hungary for two years. With Ottoman assistance, the traitor Zápolya established effective control over all the country except a fringe to the north and west, which remained under the control of Louis's brother-in-law Ferdinand of Habsburg.

The defeat at Mohács ended Hungary as a single independent state for generations. All western Europe was horrified, but also aware of its collective failure; despite increasingly desperate appeals from Louis, nobody had gone to his aid. Hungary never fully recovered, and the momentous defeat entered its folklore. An old Hungarian song tells of a series of domestic disasters; after each comes the chorus, *Több is veszett Mohácsnál* – 'But no matter; more was lost on Mohács field'. And to this day, a common saying of Hungarians when faced with misfortune is, 'More was lost at Mohács.'

Chapter 5

Barbarossa; the 1565 Siege of Malta; the conquest of Cyprus; the Battle of Lepanto; the 1683 Siege of Vienna

Influential German religious reformer Martin Luther, who had previously poo-pooed the existential threat to Western civilisation, now published a book, *On War against the Turk*, compelling the Habsburg crown to defend the Holy Roman Empire from Islamic expansion: 'It is a fact that the Turk is at our throat, and even if he does not will to march against us this year,' he wrote,' yet he is there, armed and ready any hour to attack us.' He wrote a prayer for deliverance from the Muslims, asking God to 'give to our emperor perpetual victory over our enemies'.

He had always seen that Muslims were a scourge but in 1518, in his *Explanation of the Ninety-five Theses*, he had argued against a religious crusade, provoking accusations of defeatism. He did support the idea of a secular war against them, however, arguing in 1526 in *Whether Soldiers can be in a State of Grace* that national defence is reason for a just war. But he emphasised that the spiritual war against the alien religion was separate, to be waged through prayer and repentance. After reading a Latin translation of the *Koran*, however, he wrote several pamphlets harshly critical of Islam, which he now regarded as a tool of Satan.

His predicted Muslim assault came in 1529, when, in a spring notable for its rainfall, Suleiman mustered a colossal army in Bulgaria that marched to besiege Vienna. As well as comprising 125,000 men, the force also contained 20,000 camels – most of whom, genetically unsuited to mud and perpetual soaking, perished on the march. Food could not be cooked in the pouring rain, nor tents pitched properly in the sodden ground. Reports say men spent nights perched in trees muttering to themselves the Turkish equivalent of, 'Sod this for a game of soldiers' and that some succumbed to sleep and fell, dropping off in both senses.

But, despite the great discomfort, they reached Vienna. And, though drenched, disgruntled and miserable, many of them ill and a third of the force being cavalry ineffective in siege warfare, they still outnumbered the defenders five to one. And many of the defenders were an ad-hoc resistance formed from local farmers, peasants and other civilians.

Suleiman sent three emissaries to the garrison with the message: 'If you become Muslims nothing will happen to you. But if you resist us, then by Allah the most sublime your city will be reduced to ashes and young and old slaughtered.' Aware of the previous atrocities committed by Muslims after they had promised mercy to any who surrendered, the garrison refused these terms.

As the Muslim army settled into position, the garrison launched sorties to disrupt the digging and mining of tunnels below the city's walls by the invaders' sappers. As at the 1453 siege of Constantinople, defenders detected underground activity by observing agitation in bowls of water placed on the walls and outworks. They detonated several Ottoman mines intended to bring down the walls, subsequently despatching 8,000 men to attack the Muslim mining operations, destroying many of the tunnels but sustaining serious losses when the confined spaces hindered their retreat. Among these casualties was the commander of the defence, Nicholas, Count of Salm, an experienced professional soldier aged 70, who was mortally wounded by a lump of falling masonry.

Yet more torrential rain came five days later, and with the Muslims failing to make any breaches in the walls, and assault attempts also failing, the prospects for victory began to fade. Also, Suleiman was facing critical shortages of supplies such as food and water; casualties, illness and desertions began taking a toll on his army's ranks; and cold weather was approaching. He realised that success was impossible and withdrew, after slaying all adult male prisoners. The Austrians vigorously pursued and harassed the retreating force. Adding to the Muslims' difficulties were premature blizzards, making the roads so muddy that all wagons and carts had to be abandoned.

Undeterred, three years later the Muslims invaded again. Suleiman led another big expedition north from Belgrade. Avoiding a confrontation with a force sent to defend Vienna, he turned into south-west Austria by way of the Mur-Drava valley. After his light cavalry had ravaged lower Austria, he withdrew down the river Drava, the campaign a dismal failure.

Suleiman continued to constantly attack towns and forts held by Ferdinand however, until signing a peace treaty with Ferdinand the next year as he was keen to devote himself to war with Persia. The 'eternal' peace agreed on conceded to Ferdinand control of the north and west strip of Hungary that was a third of the country, but exacted from Ferdinand an annual tribute. Ferdinand acknowledged Zápolya as king of Hungary as an Ottoman vassal, and the Ottomans acknowledged Habsburg rule over what was called 'Royal Hungary'.

The treaty satisfied neither Zápolya nor Ferdinand. Their armies started to skirmish along the borders and Ferdinand decided to strike a decisive blow at Zápolya. In 1537 he sent an army of 24,000 men (from Austria, Hungary, the Holy Roman Empire, Bohemia, the Tyrol and Croatia) but because of the approach of Ottoman cavalry sent as reinforcement to Zápolya by the governor of Belgrade, it had to retreat. The pursuing Ottoman army caught up with it near the marsh of Gorjani on the Drava river in present-day Slavonia (now in east Croatia). It was severely defeated, the entire force annihilated. Twenty thousand men were slain, including General Pavle Bakić, whose severed head was taken to Constantinople.

Also in 1537, a big Ottoman fleet, with corsair Khair ed-Din, known as Barbarossa, 'Redbeard', as admiral, captured several Greek islands, besieged Corfu and ravaged the Calabrian coast of southern Italy. The pope assembled a Christian alliance fleet to confront him. The fleets met in a naval battle the following year near Preveza in north-west Greece. The Muslims swiftly engaged Christian ships but Admiral Andrea Doria, Prince of Melfi, a sailor of fortune who also predominantly influenced Genoese politics, including reforming the constitution so that plebeians were declared ineligible for the doge's office, hesitated to bring his centre into action.

Barbarossa took advantage of a lack of wind that immobilised the Christian barques that accounted for most of the numerical superiority of the allies. The Muslims easily boarded the barques from their more mobile galleys and galliots. Doria's efforts to trap the Muslim ships between the cannon fire of his barques and galleys failed and the Muslims sank, destroyed or captured 128 ships, slew thousands of Christians and took about 3,000 prisoners. The Muslims lost no ships, though several were seriously damaged by the cannon fire of the massive Venetian flagship, *Galeone di Venezia*. The next morning, Doria, with a wind in his favour and unwilling to risk the Genoese ships, as he personally owned many of them, set sail for Corfu, ignoring the pleas of the other commanders to continue the fight.

Barbarossa returned the following year and captured most of the remaining Christian outposts on the Greek islands. Venice and the Ottomans then signed a treaty in which Venice had to pay the Muslims a war indemnity of 300,000 gold ducats, and the Muslims took control of the Venetian possessions in the Morea and in Dalmatia and of the formerly Venetian islands in the Aegean, Ionian and eastern Adriatic seas. In the Mediterranean in 1543 a fleet under Barbarossa bombarded, besieged and sacked Nice.

In all these waters Barbarossa's green flag had come to be a dreaded sight. It depicted a two-bladed sword representing a fearsome Islamic bifurcated scimitar of legend named Dhul-Fiqar, transliterated as Zulfikar, which was common among Ottoman soldiers and sailors as an emblem. As pictured on this flag, prominent under verse 61:13 of the *Koran*, the blades were so widely spaced apart the image looked like a compass or a pair of scissors. The crossbones behind or beneath the skull on the Jolly Roger black flags of the pirates of the following two centuries evolved from the Zulfikar on Barbarossa's flag. Originally they were crossed swords, resembling its scissor-like blades.

Naval military historian Edward Keble Chatterton wrote in 1909 that Barbarossa was the greatest pirate that ever lived, one of the cleverest tacticians and strategists the Mediterranean ever bore on its waters and that his death in 1546 'was received by Christian Europe with a sigh of the greatest relief'.

By then the Ottomans were one of three Muslim states that occupied or controlled a broad belt of lands and seas extending from Morocco, Ethiopia and the Austrian border to the fringes of Central Asia, the foothills of the Himalayas and the Bay of Bengal. All three of these major states were the creation of Turkish-speaking Muslim dynasties of a strongly military character.

And the Ottomans, after devastating much of Hungary and while waging war with Persia, continued to fight Christian forces in the Mediterranean, where Muslim fleets dominated, capturing Tripoli in 1551. Muslim expansion in north Africa followed, with most potentates in the region acknowledging Ottoman suzerainty. Suleiman added greatly to his dominions there, his conquests including Algiers.

Muslim warships and corsairs terrorised the Mediterranean. Port Mahon in Minorca was seized and sacked. The capture of the island of Djerba, off the Tunisian coast, had brought the Muslims close to Tunis, and a Christian fleet was destroyed at the Battle of Djerba in 1560. Tunis would finally be taken by the Muslims in 1574.

After the loss of Rhodes, the Order of the Knights of St John had been granted the Maltese islands and Tripoli by Holy Roman Emperor Charles the Fifth and in 1530 the knights established themselves in Malta. The annual fee was a peregrine falcon, payable on All Saints' Day, 1 November. In 1541 the Gascon knight La Valette was involved in a naval battle in which he was wounded and his ship, the *San Giovanni*, was captured. La Valette was taken as a galley slave for a year by Barbary pirates before being released in an exchange of prisoners.

In 1554 La Valette was elected captain general of the order's galleys, and, three years later, grand master. Three years after that he formed an alliance with the Habsburg empire to reconquer Tripoli but the expedition resulted in the defeat at Djerba. Despite this, the order's galleys were able to rescue several other Christian vessels and, later on in his reign, La Valette greatly strengthened the order's navy.

And, crucially, he organised the defence of Malta when, in March 1565, the Muslims attacked the island with one of the biggest fleets since antiquity. It consisted of 193 vessels, transporting 30,000 troops, including janissaries. But the defenders, ably commanded by La Valette, though heavily outnumbered, had prepared well, and reinforcements had been promised by the viceroy of Sicily, Don Garcia, who was fully aware that, if Malta fell, Italy would be the next to be invaded.

Guarding the entrance to Grand Harbour rose the towering walls of the knights' impressive redoubt of Fort St Elmo, superbly garrisoned by 150 defenders. Ottoman specialist engineers had assessed the fortification from local informants and conducting reconnaissance missions and said it would fall within three days. Their cursory examination suggested to them that, as a traditional star-shaped fort, it would not be particularly difficult to conquer. But the vastly outnumbered Christians held out for thirty-one days. After fierce fighting, by the time the Muslims seized the fort, smashing their way in, only sixty defenders remained alive. Of these, all but nine were immediately decapitated. The headless corpses were then floated across the bay on mock crucifixes. The defenders retaliated by beheading all their Muslim prisoners and firing the heads from two cannon into the ruins of the fort.

The knights managed to hold out on the headland of Birgu, their fortified town, and the narrow inlet to the south-east of the neighbouring headland of Senglea. It was on the defence of these two parallel peninsulas, surrounded by Muslim troops, that they depended on for survival.

Despite the destruction of St Elmo, the invaders could not prevail and in early September the weather turned and they marched on the town of Mdina, intending to winter there. But the poorly-defended town fired its single cannon at them, a bluff that, by fooling the already demoralised Muslims into thinking it had plenty of ammunition, scared them away. By now they had lost a third of their men to fighting and disease.

On the very day that St Elmo fell, ships from Sicily carrying a relief force of a thousand men, including forty-two knights from north Europe, had managed to land and, a week later, to make their way by night to what is now Kalkara, beyond a creek to the north-east of Birgu. Not only the arrival of the force itself, but also its almost miraculous success in avoiding the Muslim army, had an immense effect on the defenders' morale.

But the struggle continued. In mid-July a concerted Muslim attack on Senglea was made from the sea. It was foiled by the courage of native

Maltese, superb swimmers, who tipped the Muslims from their boats and fought them hand to hand in the water. A hidden gun emplacement completed the rout. On 7 August an Italian gunner named Francesco Balbi di Correggio, who later penned a fascinating eyewitness account of the siege, wrote:

> General assault – 8,000 on St Michael's [a small fortress], 4,000 on the port of Castile... But when they left their trenches we were already at our posts, the hoops alight, the pitch boiling... When they scaled the works they were received like men who were expected... The assault lasted nine hours, from daybreak till after noon, during which the Muslims were relieved by fresh troops more than a dozen times, while we refreshed ourselves with drinks of well-watered wine and some mouthfuls of bread... Victory was given us again... though not one of us could stand on his feet for wounds or fatigue.

By now the Muslim troops, too, were weakening. The heat was merciless. Water was short since the dead animals with which the knights had deliberately fouled the springs had been supplemented by many Muslim corpses. By the end of August dysentery had spread through the Muslim camp, its victims being carried in the blazing sun to the improvised sick tents where they died in their hundreds. The Muslims began to retreat.

The men of the *Grande Soccorso* (Great Relief) had positioned themselves and when some hot-heads among them saw the retreat and the burning villages in its wake, they charged without waiting for orders, which led to a general charge that resulted in a massacre of the retreating Muslims. The few surviving Muslims fled to the sea, which was soon red with their blood. Those who managed to board their ships briefly contemplated a counter-attack but they had lost too many men and supplies and morale was low and they sailed away.

Thanks to the heroism of La Valette's knights, Malta had survived the Muslim assault. The Christians had suffered terrible losses. Two hundred and fifty knights were dead, most of the survivors wounded. Birgu, the capital, had been razed. Vulnerable to fire on every side, strategically it had proved a disaster. And so when old La Valette limped forward to lay the first stone of a new capital, he did so not on the ruins of the old one but away on the heights opposite, dominating Grand Harbour. As he richly deserved, the new capital was named after him: Valletta. Nobody knows where the extra 'l' came from.

Throughout Europe people celebrated what turned out to be the last epic battle involving Crusader knights. Voltaire said, 'Nothing is better known than the siege of Malta.' Queen Elizabeth had written, 'If the Turks should prevail against the Isle of Malta, it is uncertain what further peril might follow to the rest of Christendom.' Suleiman, anticipating victory, had spoken of invading Europe through Italy but his string of victories, and further expansion, ended with his defeat on Malta.

It was his only decisive defeat. He died in his tent in Austria aged 71 on his thirteenth military campaign after yet another siege, when he was overcome with excitement at the news of the gory death of an enemy. Suleiman had been carried to the battle on a litter because of gout. Called 'the Magnificent', he was regarded as the greatest of the sultans. Thirty years after his death 'Sultan Solyman' was known by Shakespeare and mentioned in *The Merchant of Venice*. Among his many awesome accomplishments, apart from the deaths of hundreds of thousands of civilians and soldiers in his military campaigns, and the suffering of millions more, were the murders of a finance secretary, a grand vizier who had been a childhood friend, two of his sons and four grandsons.

His original plan on the Austrian campaign had been to march on the town of Eylau, which controlled the route leading into Transylvania; but while he was still in Belgrade he received a report that the ruler of the town of Szeged, Count Nicholas Zriny, had slain one of his top officials. This clearly could not be allowed to go unpunished, and he immediately ordered his army to march on the town. He followed. Ninety thousand men awaited him.

The siege of Szeged took a month. The town itself was quickly burnt down and resistance thereafter was confined to the fortress, where Zriny held out until all the outer bastions were held by the Muslims and he and 600 remaining men were surrounded in the central keep. He then dressed up, 'as if for a feast', it was said, and marched out for a heroic but suicidal last stand. Few of his men survived and he himself was badly wounded. He was not permitted to die of his wounds. His head was rammed into the mouth of a Muslim cannon just before it was fired.

It was the exciting report of this gruesome death that caused Suleiman's own demise. New grand vizier Mehmed Sokollu acted fast, realising that it was vital to ensure the peaceful succession of Suleiman's son Selim, a drunken debauchee who was the sole remaining heir to the Ottoman empire. He sent a messenger to Selim, urging him to come at full speed.

Sokollu was fully aware that once the army – and particularly the janissaries – got to know of Suleiman's death, all discipline would collapse and there would be chaos in the camp. Therefore the few who were already aware of it, including the doctors, were swiftly executed. He announced that Suleiman was suffering from a severe attack of gout, and had asked him to temporarily assume the supreme authority.

He took into his confidence just one man, the chief standard-bearer, who was later to marry his daughter. This man was a gifted forger who could imitate Suleiman's signature to perfection. The generals, continuing to receive their daily orders just as they always had, suspected nothing; letters went out to the princes of Europe, the shah of Persia, the khan of the Crimea, the Ottoman provincial governors – all of them signed with Suleiman's usual flourish, announcing his victory.

Another missive was sent to the governor of Buda, enclosing the small pieces of what little remained of Zriny's head.

The army remained in the camp for forty-three days, with heavily armed sentries continually on guard outside Suleiman's tent preventing all but Sokollu from entering. Only then did Sokollu give the order to depart. He announced that Suleiman would travel in a closed litter. An Ottoman chronicler wrote:

> From time to time Sokollu approached the throne, pretending to make a report to the sultan. He also gave the impression of discussing the report with him after he had read it out… Many

rumours were circulating, but the skilful tactics of the grand vizier managed to dissipate suspicions.

Nobody knew for sure whether Suleiman was dead or alive.

Selim had left immediately on receiving Sokollu's letter and met his father's clandestine funeral cortège as it approached Belgrade. Only then did Sokollu reveal to the army as a whole that Suleiman had indeed died. Summoning the professional readers of the *Koran*, he bade them recite the appropriate prayers. The full funeral service started just before dawn the next morning.

The army was already grumbling. By long tradition the janissaries and other regiments received 'accession gifts' whenever one sovereign succeeded another. Only after these had duly been distributed were the recipients sufficiently appeased to continue their march, though still unhappy at the inadequacy of the distribution. And violence broke out when they reached Constantinople. Two top officials – the chief admiral and the second vizier – were dragged from their horses and beaten; Sokollu himself escaped by throwing gold coins at his assailants. Order was restored only after some executions and a promise from Selim that the janissaries' pay would be substantially increased.

Selim the Second was nicknamed 'the Sot'. And he was not only a great drinker but also a great womaniser. His princely *harem* at Magnesia in the Ottomans' Aegean region was said to be comparable to the *harem* in Jannah, the Islamic paradise, in its assemblage of beautiful females. Selim was so possessive of it that he had a friend named Gazanfer castrated in order that Gazanfer could serve in it. (Gazanfer's younger brother was also castrated but did not survive the ghastly operation.)

Prominent in this brothel with her beauty and extraordinary intelligence was a local Greek girl later named Nurbanu. In three successive years she gave birth by Selim to two daughters and her only son, Murad, and she became the new sultan's favourite wife, whom he consulted on all major issues.

Because he was away invading other lands most of the time, this made her extremely powerful. She and Sokollu controlled much of state affairs. Two years after Selim's accession they concluded at Constantinople a treaty with the Holy Roman Emperor, Maximilian the Second, in which the emperor agreed to pay an annual tribute of 30,000 gold ducats and granted the Ottomans authority in Moldavia and Wallachia.

This perk encouraged Nurbanu and Sokollu to draw up a plan to join the Volga and Don by a canal to facilitate Ottoman authority in the region, and in the summer of the following year a big force was sent to besiege Astrakhan by the Volga delta and start the canal works, while a fleet besieged Azov. A sortie from the Astrakhan garrison first drove back the delta besiegers, then a Russian relief army of 15,000 attacked and scattered the workmen and the Tatar force sent for their protection; and then the fleet was destroyed by a storm. Early in 1570 Russian ambassadors in Constantinople concluded a peace treaty.

Thwarted in their plan for the east, Nurbanu and Sokollu concentrated on invading Cyprus. The invasion took place later that year.

Cyprus, which had been under Venetian rule since 1489, had an indigenous Greek population of 160,000. Apart from its strategic location in the eastern Mediterranean between the Ottoman heartland of Anatolia and the newly acquired provinces of the Levant and Egypt, the island possessed a profitable production of cotton and sugar. The Venetians, to safeguard their most distant colony, had paid an annual tribute of 8,000 ducats to the Mamluke sultans of Egypt, and after the Ottomans destroyed the Mamlukes the agreement was renewed with the Ottomans. Nurbanu did not believe that Venice would continue with this treaty. Sokollu disagreed and thought breaching it unjustified. Nurbanu's opinion prevailed, a juridical court ruling that a breach of the treaty was justified because Cyprus was a 'former land of Islam' and had to be retaken. For thirty-four years in the seventh century Arabs had ruled Cyprus. This was before their new religion was even called Islam. Their garrison was withdrawn after Byzantine emperor Constantine the Fourth defeated it. Muslims have always regarded as eternally theirs any land they once ruled, no matter how briefly or long ago. Money for the new campaign was raised by the confiscation and resale of monasteries and churches of the Greek Orthodox Church in Ottoman territory.

The Ottoman commander, Lala Mustafa, a former tutor of Selim, drew up his vastly superior army to surround Nicosia, which had demolished everything outside its walls to provide clear fields of fire for its artillery. After a six-week siege, the invaders stormed the defences and slaughtered its 20,000 inhabitants.

Kyrenia avoided the same fate by surrendering quickly but Famagusta's 8,000-man garrison kept Mustafa's force of 200,000 men at bay for ten months before the survivors gave in after being re-assured they could leave Cyprus freely. But Mustafa, angry at having lost 52,000 men in the siege, broke his word, imprisoning them, and the Venetian general, Marco Bragadin, who was mutilated by having his nose and ears cut off, briefly imprisoned and then flayed alive and his corpse hung on Mustafa's galley together with the heads of three other Venetian officers. Bragadin's skin was then paraded around the island before being sent to Constantinople. The Cathedral of Nicholas in Famagusta became a mosque named after Mustafa.

(In Shakespeare's tragedy *Othello*, the only one set in his own age, the Bard brazenly uses poetic licence to portray Othello as the general who was sent from Venice to defend Cyprus at the time of the Ottoman invasion.)

Mustafa's barbaric treatment of Bragadin was a factor in Christian leaders' determined response to the conquest. The pope had been establishing a fleet of a coalition of southern European Catholic maritime states to relieve Famagusta but the forces had been too slow to gather, due to mutual suspicions of Spain and Venice. Bragadin's gruesome fate strengthened their resolve; shelving their differences, under the command of Don Juan of Austria they speeded up their preparations to confront the rampaging Muslims.

Turkish admiral Ali Monizindade had been ravaging Venetian possessions in the Aegean and Ionian seas, then his fleet had sailed into the Adriatic to within sight of Venice: learning of the increased Christian naval preparations, he rushed back to the Ionian Sea, where the naval Battle of Lepanto took place on 7 October 1571 on the northern edge of the Gulf of Corinth.

The Christian fleet's cannon were made by gunmaker Beretta, a company that had been in the same family for forty-five years and to this day has a shop in central London's Jermyn Street. Though small and few, mounted in the bow of the galleys they were lethal and decisive, for few of the Muslims were wearing armour. Neither side had a tactical plan other than a crude mêlée, to be won by ramming and boarding. The Christians had 227 ships and 84,000 men, the Muslims 270 slightly smaller vessels and about 88,000 men.

The allied Christian fleet defeated the Muslim fleet in four hours of fighting in which 30,000 men died. The sea was full of corpses. Survivors remembered the scene as a vision of the Apocalypse. The Muslims lost sixty galleys that went aground, fifty-three sunk and 117 captured, with more than 20,000 men slain or drowned, the local population slaughtering many who swam ashore from their sinking ships. The Christians lost thirteen galleys, with 7,566 dead and almost 8,000 wounded, including Miguel Cervantes, the author of *Don Quixote*, the world's first modern novel, who received three severe gunshot wounds, two in the chest and one that left his left hand permanently maimed. He spent six months in hospital and medical records show that two years later his chest wounds were still not completely healed.

News of the victory reached the Spanish king, Philip the Second, on 31 October, the message, having travelled 2,175 miles at ninety-three miles a day using the efficient chain of relay stations across Europe, taking a record three weeks. As it was All Souls' Day he was at prayer, and ordered the choir to immediately sing the *Te Deum*, the ancient Latin hymn used as an expression of thanks on special occasions. His chief minister hailed the victory as 'the greatest naval victory since the pharaoh's army drowned in the Red Sea'.

Two months later Philip's son and short-lived heir apparent Ferdinand was born and the coincidence led him to pardon all prisoners in his jails and to commission from the most famous painter of his day, Titian, a huge painting that commemorated the two events. (Ferdinand died of dysentery aged seven.)

The defeat of the Muslims was well worth a *Te Deum*. They naturally played it down, arguing that it caused no lasting harm to the Ottoman empire, while the capture of Cyprus by the Ottomans was a significant blow to Christianity. Sokollu said to a Venetian emissary:

You come to see how we bear our misfortune. But I would have you know the difference between your loss and ours. In wresting Cyprus from you, we deprived you of an arm; in defeating our fleet, you have only shaved our beard. An arm when cut off cannot grow again; but a shorn beard will grow all the better for the razor.

He shrugged off the defeat with a euphemistic 'the battle of the dispersed fleet', even though the Muslim fleet had in fact not been dispersed but annihilated. Had the battle not been fought and lost, in the spring the fleet would have left its anchorages in the gulf and probably conquered the nearby Venetian outposts in the Adriatic or even taken Crete. The defeat prevented the Ottoman empire expanding further along the European side of the Mediterranean (though Ottoman suzerainty was established over the entire southern coast). Once again, as happened several times throughout history, only a Muslim defeat in a desperate battle prevented western Europe from being over-run by Islam. Cervantes said, 'It was the greatest day's work in centuries.' The destroyed Muslim ships became driftwood collected on beaches. Ornate pieces were kept as decoration, the rest chopped up for firewood.

Lepanto was the last major naval battle in the Mediterranean fought entirely between galleys. It demonstrated even to the victors the decisive impact of new technology against the most sophisticated, seasoned and formidable enemy in naval battles, and galleys, though still used for a while as transports and as auxiliaries to broadside-battery sailing ships, ceased to be used in actual fighting. During the previous decades there had been unprecedented revolution in naval warfare. The era of the galley, which had lasted for more than 2,000 years, ended as the potentialities of naval gunfire were realised and exploited.

Sea tactics had not changed since those by which the Greeks had defeated the Persians in the Battle of Salamis in 480 BC. Galleys of 1571 were similar to those used by the Romans in the Punic Wars. They were primarily a floating fort or platform, carrying soldiers who were to engage other soldiers on enemy vessels. Naval battles were essentially fought like ground combat as soon as the enemy ships came within the range of archery or light cannon. The conflict culminated in the ramming (for which purpose a metal beak projected forward from just above the water line), boarding and capturing of an enemy vessel.

Early in the sixteenth century a shipwright in the French port of Brest named Descharges had invented an opening with a hinged cover in the side of ships facilitating the stowage of cargo in the hull without hoisting overside. English shipbuilders, spurred by Henry VIII's determination to mount heavy guns in his planned new warships, seized on the idea as a way to permit a cannon to be fired from the lower decks of a vessel. And so the gun port and broadside battery came into existence. The Spanish eventually followed suit. The resulting warship was called a galleon, because, like the galley, it was a ship designed specifically for war. Its row of big cannon in the main hull gave galleons the ability to fight at long range without necessarily closing for the traditional hand-to-hand climax of earlier naval engagements. Rather than wasting space and manpower by carrying a garrison of landlubber soldiers, sailors were trained to scramble down the rigging and pick up a cutlass when the time came to board an enemy ship or to repel boarders. Thus came into being a new type of fighting man, the marine.

G.M. Trevelyan, in his 1942 *English Social History*, wrote that, by the broadside – the rows of cannon protruding between the timbers – sea warfare was completely changed:

> It ceased to be a game of soldiers seeking to grapple their ship to the enemy and fight deck to deck as if on land; it became, instead, a game of sailors, manoeuvring their ship so as to fire her cannon with most effect. The ship ceased to be a platform for a storming-party and became a moving battery of guns.

He added:

> This change in the character of warfare at sea was better understood and more quickly exploited by the English than by the Spanish, who had Mediterranean traditions connected with the oared galley and the grappling of ship to ship. These ancient and honourable traditions hampered Spanish seamanship, even after

Philip improvised an ocean-going navy to conquer England in the Atlantic and the [English] Channel. His Armada [1588] was, in its real spirit, an army embarked; the soldiers outnumbered and bullied the sailors, regarding them as drudges whose privilege it was to bring the gallant *soldado* to grips with his enemies. In contrast, in the English fleet the captains were seamen and they were in full command of everyone on board. Francis Drake, on his voyage round the world [1577-80], established the rule that even the gentleman volunteer must haul at the ropes with the sailor.

After Lepanto the Muslims eventually built a replacement fleet of exactly the same size, containing 134 galleys, but building sturdy galleys took a long time. An eyewitness wrote that a close look at the new fleet revealed ships of green timber provided with cannon hastily cast. In theory, this fleet could have sailed to replace the one destroyed at Lepanto, resume the depredations of Venetian possessions and approach Venice, as its predecessor had done. But it never set sail. In practice, it was not fit for purpose, and most of the galleys remained in port as decaying hulks, maritime follies.

Muslim galleys were similar to those of the Christians, the main difference being that the Christian ships had a shielding screen called a mantelot to protect their oarsmen. The Turks did not bother. Their galley slaves, despised expendable infidels, were defenceless – chained to their benches and fully exposed to enemy fire.

At Lepanto, probably about 10,000 European galley slaves went down with their ships. Another 15,000 were freed from captured or sinking Muslim vessels. The horror from which these were released is beyond comprehension. The conditions in which Ottoman galley slaves were kept are unimaginable. Simon Webb graphically describes them in his excellent book *The Forgotten Slave Trade: The White European Slaves of Islam*:

> A typical galley might have twenty-five oars on each side and perhaps three to five rowers for each oar. To ensure that the ship moved forward at the correct speed, every one of those rowers

would need to be seated on his bench and rowing at all times that the vessel was travelling. For this reason, the slaves were shackled in place and were therefore physically unable to move from their designated position. Keeping them chained constantly in one place served two important purposes. First, as we have said, it meant that every oar would be working at full strength at all time, but there was another good reason not to allow the slaves to wander about at will. This is that with around fifty oars to a boat and sometimes as many as five rowers to each oar, it was not uncommon to have 250 slaves who had absolutely nothing to lose on board a galley. The chances of a revolt by such a large body of desperate men were always present in the minds of those commanding the ship. Far safer simply to keep them shackled permanently in their places. This meant that when the need arose to urinate or defecate, these men had no option but to do so where they were sitting.

It was said in the sixteenth century that a galley crewed by slaves could be smelled from as far away as a mile (Bridge, 1988). A moment's thought will soon confirm that this was unlikely to be an exaggeration. Imagine, if you will, hundreds of men confined in a narrow space and compelled by nature to open their bladders and bowels where they were seated, day in and day out, for years at a time. There was no provision for washing and so these men would never have the chance to wash off the stale sweat from their bodies and if any activity is likely to generate copious amounts of sweat, it is propelling a large and heavily laden ship through the ocean by muscle-power alone. The rowers spent their lives ankle-deep in human waste.

For security they were never unshackled from their benches, so had to sleep as best they could, sitting upright, unable to stretch out. And when they became too weak to row, for whatever reason, they were thrown overboard to drown.

Cervantes himself spent five years as a Muslim slave after a ship he was on was attacked by Barbary Coast corsairs. Recently discovered Turkish evidence suggests that, despite having lost the movement of his left hand, for a time he worked on a construction site in Constantinople. Following four escape attempts, he was ransomed by the Trinitarians, a religious order founded with the object of freeing prisoners of the Muslims. During the era that the Barbary corsairs were seizing prisoners wholesale across Europe, the Trinitarians begged money from all who could give it, so that they might negotiate the release of slaves for cash. In time, this ransoming of slaves proved more of a money-spinner for the corsairs than simply selling those they caught on the open slave market. People would be prepared to pay up to a certain amount for a healthy slave but there was no limit to what a loving family would pay to recover a husband, father or son. For decades, these corsairs did as they pleased in the Mediterranean, the eastern Atlantic, the North Sea and the English Channel.

King James I, who succeeded Elizabeth, was not interested in the Royal Navy, and neglected it to such an extent that the fleet which, under her reign, had routed the mighty Spanish Armada was no longer able even to protect English fishing boats from the depredations of the corsairs. For more than half a century, English fishermen, with no navy to defend them, risked being seized and taken to a Muslim slave market.

Between 1609 and 1616, 466 English ships were boarded and the crews carried off into slavery. In April 1625 three Cornish ships and one sailing from Dartmouth were captured by corsairs and their crews taken. The following month, an entry in the *Calendar of State Papers* read, 'The Turks are upon our coasts. They take ships only to take the men to make slaves of them.' (Because the corsairs were Muslims in the Ottoman empire they were habitually referred to as 'Turks'.) In August the Plymouth mayor wrote to the privy council in London pleading for help from the Royal Navy because twenty-seven ships had been captured by corsairs in ten days, with all 200 of the men on board them enslaved.

And not only were vessels seized – the Royal Navy could not stop Muslim slavers actually landing on British soil and taking people on to their ships to be transported to the slave markets. Also in August 1625 a raiding party landed on the coast of Cornwall. Villagers saw the ships at anchor and fled to the church, to no avail. The slavers dragged sixty of them from the church, loaded them into their rowing boats and took them on board the waiting ships. They all ended up in the slave markets of north Africa. The Kent and Sussex coasts were also obvious and tempting frequent targets; as was the Irish village of Baltimore in West Cork where, in 1631, 109 people were taken away and endured a journey of thirty-eight days before arriving in Algiers, where they were sold to the highest bidder. Some of the men ended up as galley slaves, the children were separated from their mothers and forcibly converted to Islam, and many of the women were forced into a *harem*. Only three women ever made it back to Ireland. After the raid, the remaining villagers moved to a bigger settlement further inland. The site of Baltimore was deserted for generations, becoming desolation.

In 1840 writer Thomas Davis wrote a poem about the raid entitled *The Sacking of Baltimore*, in which one verse reads:

All, all asleep within each roof along that rocky street,
And these must be the lover's friends, with gently gliding feet –
A stifled gasp, a dreamy noise! 'The roof is in a flame!'
From out their beds and to their doors rush maid and sire and dame,
And meet upon the threshold stone the gleaming sabre's fall,
And o'er black and bearded face the white or crimson shawl.
The yell of 'Allah!' breaks above the prayer, and shriek, and roar:
O blessed God! The Algerine is lord of Baltimore!

As well as underfunding, the Royal Navy had another problem in that its ships were big, heavily-armed vessels built for conventional naval warfare. They were neither fast enough nor adequately manoeuvrable to deal with swift attacks of small groups of ships darting in and out of British waters. The boldness and frequency of the raids on Britain and other parts of Europe were extraordinary. Sometimes, more than one ship would be attacked simultaneously.

After 1619, destitute Moriscos who had been expelled from Spain had settled in Morocco at a seaport near its capital, Rabat. Having no money and no means of acquiring any, they adopted piracy as a source of income. This seaport was called Salé. The sultan of Morocco allowed the newcomers to settle there because he made a deal with them in which they paid him ten per cent of their booty, either in slaves or treasure. So the bizarre republic of Salé was founded, a small enclave in Morocco specialising in piracy.

Novelist Daniel Defoe describes a thrilling naval fight in which Robinson Crusoe is captured and enslaved by these corsairs:

> Our ship... was surprised in the grey of the morning by a Turkish rover of Sallee, who gave chase to us with all the sail she could make. We crowded also as much canvas as our yards would spread, or our masts carry, to have got clear; but finding the pirate gained upon us, and would certainly come up with us in a few hours, we prepared to fight; our ship having twelve guns, and the rogue eighteen. About three in the afternoon he came up with us, and bringing to, by mistake, just athwart our quarter, instead of athwart our stern, as he intended, we brought eight of our guns to bear on that side and poured in a broadside upon him, which made him sheer off again, after returning our fire and pouring in also his small shot from near two hundred men which he had on board. However, we had not a man touched, all our men keeping close. He prepared to attack us again, and we to defend ourselves; but laying us on board the next time upon our other quarter, he entered sixty men upon our decks, who immediately fell to cutting and hacking the decks and rigging. We plied them with small shot, half-pikes, powder chests, and such like, and cleared our deck of them twice. However, to cut short this melancholy part of our story, our ship being disabled, and three of our men killed and eight wounded, we were obliged to yield, and were carried all prisoners into Sallee, a port belonging to the Moors.
>
> The usage I had there was not so dreadful as at first I apprehended, nor was I carried up the country to the emperor's court, as the rest of our men were, but was kept by the captain of the rover as his proper prize, and made his slave, being young and nimble, and fit for his business. At this surprising change of my circumstances, from a merchant to a miserable slave, I was perfectly overwhelmed; and now I looked back upon my father's

prophetic discourse to me, that I should be miserable and have none to relieve me, which I thought was now so effectually brought to pass that I could not be worse; for now the hand of Heaven had overtaken me, and I was undone without redemption; but alas! this was but a taste of the misery I was to go through, as will appear in the sequel of this story.

(Crusoe escapes after two years, becomes a planter in Brazil and only after that, on 1 September 1659, 'an evil hour', does he set sail on the voyage that ends with the famous fictional shipwreck and his survival marooned on a remote island for twenty-eight years.)

Simon Webb describes some raids on Britain:

In 1634, two ships carrying goods from Minehead in Somerset to Ireland were attacked and the crews captured. At other times, the African ships would work like a wolfpack to take a ship which they had targeted. On 20 September 1635, what were described as 'six Sali men-of-war' seized a ship near the Scilly Isles, which lie off the westernmost tip of Cornwall (Eliot, 1881). The following March it was reported that thirty-six ships from England, Scotland and Ireland had been taken and in June that year three fishing boats containing over fifty men had been captured 'between Falmouth and the Lizard' (Eliot, 1881). In August 1638 it was reported that 'Turkish men-of-war of Algiers' were operating in the English Channel.

Webb notes that the fact that the ships slipping in and out of British territorial water unopposed were being described as 'men-of-war' is significant. This was the term applied only to warships and not generally to pirate vessels: 'The English at the time recognized that these raids were tantamount to an act of war and that the ships were really representatives of a hostile foreign power; namely the Ottoman Empire.' Renowned French historian Fernand Braudel wrote in 1949 in his influential first book *The Mediterranean and the Mediterranean World in the Age of Philip II* that such piracy was 'a secondary form of war'.

The plundering corsairs were conducting a marine *jihad*. As always and everywhere, their *jihad*, as well as being holy, was also a nice little earner.

These naval attacks on western Europe were a counterpoint to Ottoman expansion on land. At the same time as these raids were taking place Ottoman armies were invading east and central Europe. In August 1595 a famous battle took place in Wallachia, where, south of the village of Călugăreni, a Wallachian force of 16,000 men led by Michael the Brave fought an Ottoman army more than twice as big. Michael the Brave, knowing he was heavily outnumbered, placed his force at a muddy swamp as that would negate the Muslims' military superiority. A narrow bridge over the marsh was the only crossing point. The battle lasted three days, and ended with routed Muslims and pursuing Wallachians falling together from the overcrowded bridge and wrestling in the mud.

The defeated Ottomans lost 15,000 men but after the battle an even bigger Ottoman army approached and Michael the Brave retreated that night in order to refit and regroup for more battles. Transylvanian, Habsburg and Italian fighters came from Transylvania in the north and joined his army, reinforcements that enabled him to drive out the Ottoman forces in the subsequent battles of Târgoviște (18 October) and Bucharest (22 October), both of which had been abandoned to them, and to win a battle at Giurgiu (26 October).

By then Mehmed the Third was the Ottoman sultan, having ascended to the throne on 15 January. He had immediately ordered that all his nineteen brothers be executed. They were strangled by royal executioners who, to guarantee total loyalty, by tradition were mutes. The princes were buried at a funeral service conducted with great pomp and ceremony befitting their high rank. Mass fratricide was so common among Muslim rulers on taking power because their predecessor usually had dozens of children with his several wives and his concubines.

In October of the following year Mehmed led an Ottoman army in an invasion of north Hungary, where it was victorious against a combined Christian force under the joint command of Archduke Maximillian the Third of Austria and Prince Sigismund Bathory of Transylvania at the three-day Battle of Kerestes after defeat seemed certain. The

Christian force extensively used early firearms and, positioned in fortified trenches, succeeded in driving back Ottoman assaults with a barrage of fire from muskets and cannon. Towards the end of the first day of the battle Mehmed wanted to withdraw his mauled forces but was persuaded to continue the conflict into a second day. On the next day the fighting intensified, with the Christians still winning. Christian troops actually reached Mehmed's tent. While some were trying to enter it, others, instead of continuing the engagement went in search of booty and plunder in the Ottoman camp, allowing Mehmed's élite guard of janissaries to repel the attack. The Christians at the tent retreated, and the cries of, 'The Christian enemy is fleeing!' were heard by the Ottoman troops still fighting what seemed like a losing battle on the front line. The boost of morale gained them the initiative. With a major action from the artillery, the Ottomans launched an assault across the entire front and, outflanking the Christian forces, routed them.

After the Battle of Kerestes both armies avoided such large-scale pitched battles because of the unpredictability of their outcome. Both sides focused more on smaller battles revolving around key fortresses. After 1598 the balance began to tip to the advantage of the Ottomans. Repeated attempts by the Habsburgs to recapture Buda, the capital of Ottoman Hungary, failed whereas the Ottomans captured the mighty fortress of Kanisa and managed to keep it against all odds. Danubian principalities rebelling against Turkish domination could not withstand the sheer weight of the war and one by one gave up. The Ottomans reconquered strategic Estergon. They were unable to exploit their success effectively however because of the collapse of their eastern frontier defensive system against a new offensive by their other arch enemy – the Safavid Persians.

Throughout the sixteenth century the Ottomans had fought recurring wars against the Persians, usually winning with superior powerful armies. At the end of the century the Persians, under the leadership of Muslim ruler Shah Abbas the First, built a modern army, balanced between cavalry, infantry and artillery and ready to seek vengeance.

Abbas was helped by twenty-six European adventurers, including Robert Shirley, an English artillery expert. Abbas's attitude was in marked contrast to that of his grandfather, who had expelled English traveller Anthony Jenkinson from his court on hearing he was a Christian. Abbas said he 'preferred the dust from the soles of the lowest Christian to the highest Ottoman personage'. Soon an excellent artillery organisation was created. Abbas greatly increased the number of cannon at his disposal so that he could field 500 in a single battle. With a strong contingent of musket-armed infantry and a new cavalry force, a formidable military power grew in west Asia, anxious to settle old scores with the Ottomans.

After a particularly arrogant series of demands from the Ottoman ambassador, Abbas had him seized, had his beard shaved and sent it to his master, the sultan, in Constantinople. This was effectively a declaration of war. In the resulting conflict, Abbas first recaptured Nahavand and destroyed the fortress in the town, which the Ottomans had planned to use as an advance base for attacks. The next year Abbas pretended he was setting off on a hunting expedition with his men. This was merely a ruse to deceive the Ottoman spies in his court – his target was Azerbaijan. He changed course for Kazvin, where he assembled a big army and set off to retake Tabriz, which was in Ottoman hands. For the first time, the Persians made great use of their artillery, and the town – which had been ruined by Ottoman occupation – soon fell. After the capture of Tabriz, Abbas paraded the severed heads of Ottoman soldiers on poles through the town. He then besieged Yerevan, a town that had become one of the main Ottoman strongholds in the Caucasus since the Safavids had ceded it in 1590. It finally fell in June 1604 and with it the Ottomans lost the support of most Armenians, Georgians and other Caucasians. But Abbas was unsure how the Ottomans would respond and withdrew from the region using scorched earth tactics. For a year, neither side made a move, but on 6 November 1605 the Persians, led by Abbas, scored a decisive victory near Tabriz.

The Ottoman-Safavid War of 1603-18 resulted in Ottoman defeats in all its stages. By the end of it Abbas had regained possession of Transcaucasia and Dagestan, as well as swathes of east Anatolia and Mesopotamia. The janissaries were so disgruntled by this stain on their honour they became unbearably disobedient and the sultan tried to disband them. So they strangled him with a bowstring.

They had also been disturbed by heavy losses in their corps in recent decades. According to Ottoman pay lists and treasury account books, so many janissaries died in the frequent and prolonged invasions of other lands in the sixteenth century that the number of levied boys increased from 3,000 per annual collection in the early years to more than 7,000 in the 1560s.

Regulations governing the collection of boys based on their social status and physical and mental condition were recorded in the 1606 *Laws of the Janissaries* written by a former janissary, reflecting both early practices and recent changes. Officials charged with collecting the boys could not take the only child of a family, because the head of a household needed his help to cultivate the land and hence pay his taxes. Also excluded from the child levy were the sons of village elders, as 'elders are vile and so are their children'; the sons of shepherds and herdsmen, as they had been brought up in the mountains and so lacked education; the sons of craftsmen, because they too soft to fulfil the duties for soldier's pay; married youths; orphans; those who were circumcised, for this meant they could have been Muslims, who were not allowed to be enslaved; those who were too tall or too short, as they were considered stupid or troublemakers respectively; and, before 1453, those who had visited Constantinople and returned to their province, 'for they were shameless'. Some ethnic groups, including Hungarians and Croatians, were excluded because they were considered unreliable. And some boys avoided the levy because their families bribed the recruiting officers.

Ottoman administrators compiled two copies of a detailed register for each batch of 200 boys, called 'the flock'. The register listed the boy's name, his father's name, his village and gave a physical description of the boy. The 'flock' then walked to the capital. Many died on the long journey, while others escaped.

Those who reached the capital were inspected, converted to Islam and circumcised. The most intelligent were selected for education in the palace school, where they received an excellent education and in due course could reach the highest offices in the empire. Others were given to Ottoman dignitaries. But most of the levied boys were hired out to farmers to become 'accustomed to hardship' and learn the basics of the Turkish language and Islamic customs. All were 'delivered by name and written down in a book' so they could be summoned when vacancies in the Janissary corps occurred. Government inspectors made an annual inspection of them, collecting a fee for this from the family on whose farm the boy was working. After eight years of hard work in the fields, the boys joined the ranks of janissary novices and lived in their barracks under strict military discipline. Some also served as a cheap workforce on state building sites, while others worked in the imperial gardens or in the dockyards as caulkers, hammermen, oar-makers or carpenters. Yet others began their apprenticeship in the imperial cannon foundry or the imperial naval arsenal. Only after several years of such service did the novices become fully-fledged janissaries or fill vacancies in the corps of artillery gunners, bombardiers, gun-carriage drivers or armourers. By then, they had long forgotten their family, native language and homeland.

The next sultan, Murad the Fourth, was also assassinated – by his mother! She had him poisoned. He was only 27. Because he was a known alcoholic it was put about he died of cirrhosis of the liver, which is impossible in one so young, no matter how heavy a drinker.

The mother was called Kösem, meaning 'Leader of the Herd', indicating her leadership and political intelligence, though, like Nurbanu, she was originally a Greek slave, and her name was Anastasia. At the age of 15 she was sent to the *harem* of Sultan Ahmed the First. During Murad's reign she was literally the power behind the throne, for at cabinet meetings attended by him she would sit behind him hidden from view by a curtain. Murad's successor was his brother, who was called Deli Ibrahim, 'Ibrahim the Imbecile', because of his mental condition and behaviour. At the instigation of the grand vizier, he was deposed and then strangled with a silk cord in a palace courtyard watched by officials from a window. Kösem was complicit in the murder of this son also.

Ibrahim's six-year-old son Mehmed was made sultan – the fourth Sultan Mehmed. When he grew up, Mehmed IV resumed the Muslim invasions of Europe. In early 1672 peaceful and serene Poland awoke to a horrifying reality. News from the south of the country was apocalyptic.

A vast invasion force of 300,000 Ottomans joined by 40,000 Tatars and Cossacks was advancing on the southern stronghold of Kaminets, looting and burning towns and villages on the way. The fortress, though extensive and well-positioned on high ground, was mostly in ruins, poorly equipped and had a garrison of only 1,500, commanded by Colonel Michał Wołodyjowski, who had retired to a monastery and was recalled to active service to take charge of Poland's eastern frontier defences. He was nicknamed 'the Little Knight' because of his small stature.

In August the invaders encamped on the plain below and bombarded the castle. All the defenders' senior officers except Wołodyjowski agreed on surrender. Wołodyjowski, in an act of protest, rather than witness the surrender of the fortress and to deny the Muslims the use of extra ammunition, detonated the gunpowder remaining in the castle depot, killing himself along with 800 other defenders who also refused to capitulate.

In the following year came the Battle of Khotyn, a town that had already been besieged by a Muslim army fifty years before. In this latest battle, Polish-Lithuanian forces under Polish *hetman* Jan Sobieski defeated the Ottoman forces, a charge of the most impressive cavalry in the world, the famed Polish winged hussars, chasing from the field a Muslim army fifteen times bigger. The invaders, having had their supplies and most of their artillery captured, withdrew from Poland. Sobieski and the nobles returned to Krakow as King Michael Wisniowiecki had died the day before the battle, and Sobieski was elected king.

Two years later, at the Siege of Lvov, in which Sobieski, his forces heavily outnumbered by Muslims invading yet again, ordered civilians to group conspicuously on hills, where they were handed spare lances to give the impression the number of Polish troops was much higher. This and other clever moves and tactics by Sobieski gave the Poles victory. In a surprise raid on the Muslim camp 42,000 captured hussars and dragoons were freed.

In the autumn the Muslims besieged Trembovla castle, one of the few strongholds in the region of Podolia still in Polish hands following the loss of Kaminets. Thirty thousand Muslim troops under the command of Ibrahim Shishman, 'Ibrahim the Fat', surrounded the castle, which was defended by a small unit of eighty infantry soldiers and a few members of the local nobility supported by 200 poorly armed, untrained peasants and residents of the town who had fled to the castle. Before the siege, a unit of dragoons had been stationed there but had been ordered to leave because of food shortages. Polish forces were commanded by Jan Samuel Chrzanowski, whose wife, Anna Dorota, was with him.

The defenders held their positions for a while during several assaults but shortages of food and water became severe and Chrzanowski said he was going to surrender. Anna Dorota threatened to commit suicide if he did so. Her resolve gave him courage and created an atmosphere in favour of defending the castle. She also persuaded the defenders to carry out a bold sortie, which resulted in heavy losses among the Muslims. Her determination raised morale among the Poles but their losses were also heavy. Only twenty soldiers remained who were able to fight. The Muslims did not know this, however, and, facing danger also from forces of Sobieski concentrated near Lvov, they withdrew.

These victories merely delayed the inevitable Muslim invasion of central Europe for a few years, in which time, aware that Islam still posed a mortal threat to the Christian world, Italy, Austria, Poland and the German states of Saxony and Bavaria united in an uneasy alliance, unreliable because of political squabbling.

Ever since the reign of Suleiman, the Ottomans had dreamt of conquering Vienna. For a hundred years they had patiently built roads and repaired bridges through the tributary kingdom of Hungary, planning for the inevitable day when their army would march and take the city, heralding the end of Christian dominance in Europe. The seizure of the capital of the Holy Roman Empire would, it was hoped, deal a devastating, perhaps even mortal, blow to European Christianity. Finally, on 14 July 1683, an enormous Ottoman army of more than 200,000 men arrived and besieged Vienna.

In 1676 Mehmed had appointed a new grand vizier, an Albanian who took the title of Kara Mustafa Pasha. Mehmed was usually wary of grand viziers, because of the execution of his father at the instigation of one, but he trusted Kara Mustafa and put him in command of this vast army on this crucial campaign. Kara Mustafa's plan was that after conquering Vienna he would march on to Rome and then Paris, turning their churches into mosques.

Only 20,000 soldiers defended Vienna and Kara Mustafa must have felt invincible. He was unaware that once it had become obvious that Mehmed was about to launch the long-awaited invasion in a renewed war of expansion the Christian European powers had made treaties and alliances with each other, that differences had been put aside in the face of the existential threat to Christendom.

One of these treaties was with Poland. Although Vienna had been the most likely target for Ottoman aggression, it was possible they would choose instead to attack the Poles. After all, there were already Ottoman armies in Russia and Ukraine. Poland therefore signed a mutual assistance pact whereby if Poland was attacked the Austrians would go to their aid, and if it was Vienna that was struck, then the Polish army would go to the rescue. The stage was set for a clash of civilisations, as the Christian West prepared to defend itself against its arch enemy, Islam, to decide the fate of Europe.

Vienna had a garrison of only 15,000 men and was also crippled by a severe outbreak of plague in which 76,000 had died. Vienna was a major trading crossroads between east and west and because of this traffic it had suffered more than most from the episodic plague outbreaks. In other parts of Europe the plague was called the 'Viennese Death'. Warehouses for trade goods that included clothing, fabrics, carpets, raisins, wax, lemons, rice, spices and grain were full for months at a time and heavily infested with rodents hosting fleas whose bite transmitted the disease; and Vienna was crowded and densely built.

Kara Mustafa's army surrounded it and trenches were dug up to its walls, which he knew were strong enough to withstand an artillery bombardment by his guns. The Muslims were handicapped by insufficient heavy artillery. Only a few big guns had been brought up the Danube by barge. The defending guns were superior in both quality and quantity. The Muslims were also hampered by the vigour of the defenders, who made frequent sorties. Meanwhile, Viennese ally Charles of Lorraine kept contact with the defenders via the river, and blocked Muslim raids up the Danube valley.

As digging the trenches was laborious and dangerous, European slaves were used. Sappers highly skilled in military mining, on reaching the walls through the trenches, dug tunnels under the city to convey and hold kegs of gunpowder to blow up its defensive towers. One lit fuse under the main tower was only seen and put out at the last minute, just before it reached the barrels. That blast would have decided the battle. The trenches could then also provide cover for infantry attacks after the towers had been destroyed.

Enemy miners often encountered each other in their tunnels, which grew so dense they formed a subterranean network, with chambers of keg-like rooms. When miners of the two sides met, either by chance or intentionally, because they wanted to destroy the enemy's mines or tunnels, bloody and brutal struggles ensued. Crammed together in muddy dark tunnels where they could often barely stand upright, the men blindly fought for their lives.

In early September the first mine detonated under the curtain wall. Although it was effective, some parts of the wall fell towards the ditch and slowed down the Muslim assault following the blast. This gave the defenders enough time to bar the gap with strong palisades. Shortly after, another explosion tore down a big segment of the burg-bastion. Janissaries were seen on top of the bastion but the ascent was too steep for a full-scale assault. After a couple of hours they had no choice but to give in to the defenders' steady fire. Famous military engineer Georg Rimpler, who had prepared the already formidable defences, was mortally wounded by a Muslim mine that shattered his arm.

The Muslims managed to open several breaches in the walls, and they forced their way into portions of the city, where their advance was stopped by hastily erected fortifications. By now the defenders had lost about half their strength and were running short of ammunition and other supplies and their situation seemed hopeless. Although the walls withstood the Muslims' inferior cannon fire the shells killed many defenders, and it looked as though King Sobieski was not going to honour his pledge under the alliance's defence treaty to send reinforcements.

But Kara Mustafa had made a fatal mistake. He had dismissed the possibility of being attacked from the commanding heights behind his encampment, the Kahlenberg Mountain. Indeed, the top of the mountain seemed inaccessible. No roads led there. But Sobieski, faithful to his treaty and also responding to an appeal from the pope, with an army of 45,000 men, including the winged hussars and many of the former prisoners of war freed at Lvov, reached Vienna after a forced march slowed because the winged hussars' horses were so big and cumbersome they had to be towed in carts pulled by four ordinary horses. Under cover of darkness in the night of 11 September the Poles managed to scramble up the mountain in thick mud, hauling up the cannon, the ranks inflamed and vengeful at the news that 30,000 villagers had been massacred by the Muslims after Vienna refused to surrender.

The arrival of the Poles, and their juncture with 46,000 Austrian and German allied forces, completely surprised Kara Mustafa. At dawn, his camp lay vulnerable below them, helpless before their cannon. A bombardment lasting several hours, setting the tents ablaze and offering no means of escape, preceded a massive cavalry charge, the biggest in history, led by the winged hussars on their giant horses.

And as the Polish cavalry burst into the Muslim lines and the Muslims turned to face them, the Austrian and German allied forces also charged and the garrison sallied from the city and attacked what was now the Muslim rear. During the day of the combined onslaught 40,000 Muslims were killed in their camp, while thousands more drowned in the Danube as they fled in panic and chaos, their army only escaping destruction because Sobieski, given command of all the allied forces, called off the pursuit out of fear of ambush in the dark. He sent the captured Imperial Banner of the Muslims to the pope.

After the invaders had been routed, at the end of a day's fierce fighting, an exhausted Sobieski entered Kara Mustafa's deserted tent at dusk and later wrote to his beloved French wife, Marie Casimire Louise, that Kara Mustafa's camp had been extraordinarily lavish. When defeat was inevitable Kara Mustafa had destroyed most of his belongings to deny them to the foe but some remained: 'He had baths, gardens and fountains; rabbits and cats, and a parrot that kept flying about so much we could not catch it... the vizier had also kept as a pet a marvellously beautiful ostrich – but this he had killed.'

The Polish troops came across 500 sacks of coffee beans, which they had never seen before. Mistaking the beans for camel feed, the soldiers wanted to burn them, but Sobieski let a wounded officer named Jerzy Franciszeki have them. When Sobieski's army went in pursuit of the fleeing Muslim survivors, and then helping to liberate much of northwest Hungary, Franciszeki remained in Vienna because of his wound and set up Vienna's first coffee house.

A Capuchin friar sampled the drink but found it too bitter. Deciding to try again, he flavoured it with honey and cream, thus creating cappuccino.

The croissant also dates from this time, the emperor ordering the pastry cooks to create a suitable confection in celebration. Its name comes from it being in the shape of a crescent, the Muslims' emblem. The fact that it became associated with France is ironic since the French had done nothing to help. He wanted to honour bakers because one had played an important role in the victory, when, while at his oven in a basement in the quiet of the early hours of a morning, he had heard a tunnel being dug and alerted the authorities.

Kara Mustafa, unhinged by his defeat, wildly searched for a scapegoat and executed the governor of Buda, claiming that he had been the first to flee. But the sultan was well aware of the truth and punished Kara Mustafa with the traditional Ottoman punishment for a grand vizier's failure, strangulation with a silk cord. On Christmas Day in a snowy Belgrade street the cord was put round Kara Mustafa's neck and pulled tight by men at each end, the execution witnessed by his wife and adolescent son as ordered by Mehmed.

Prominent in the Ottoman camp had been the silver-tongued Alexander Mavrocordato, a Greek who had studied at the Greek college in Rome and then at the universities of Padua and Bologna and was now the Muslims' grand dragoman, a high post that combined the duties of chief government interpreter and deputy foreign minister. On his return from the Vienna defeat he was taken to jail in chains and fined an enormous sum but his knowledge of European languages and customs made him indispensable and he was quickly reinstated.

The pope and other foreign dignitaries hailed Sobieski as the saviour of European civilisation. Over the next decade the victory at Vienna was followed by other victories. During those years Sobieski suffered from poor health and died of a heart attack in 1696, sadly not living to see the culmination of his life's work, the 1699 treaty of Karlovitz, which marked the end of Muslim control in much of central Europe and any further expansion.

Following a two-month congress between the Ottomans on one side and a coalition of the Holy Roman Empire, the Polish-Lithuanian Commonwealth, the Republic of Venice and Russia on the other, the treaty confirmed the then-current territorial holdings of each power, which meant Islam's first major territorial losses after a thousand years of invasion and conquest. In the circumstances, it could have been much worse for the Muslims. They were lucky that their chief negotiator at the talks was the smooth-talking Mavrocordato, who succeeded in making each side believe that the initiative came from the other. With just a cheerful face and a deft turn of phrase, he could relent, mollify and move on so charmingly that anger abated before it truly flared up.

For his success on this mission he was appointed *mahremi esrar*, one 'to whom secrets are discovered'. A contemporary wrote that he 'invented this new name for his office, which was never used before, nor has been since his death granted to any other'. Modern historians usually render this unique title as 'minister of the secrets' or, more intriguingly, 'intimate secretary'. This is the term used in a contemporary biography in which his associates are quoted as awarding him various epithets, from 'a handsome, discreet and civil man' to 'educated in everything and wise and practical' to 'Judas'.

For the first time in a thousand years the Muslims were compelled to negotiate from weakness rather than strength. Until the treaty of Karlovitz the diplomacy of the arrogant Ottomans had been unilateral without reciprocity. They sent no diplomats to Europe. For any discussion, European rulers and leaders were obliged to send envoys to Constantinople, where the sultan often kept them hanging about for weeks before condescending to talk to them. The Muslims were a law unto themselves, believing they were a superior people, 'the only nation on Earth', who had a divine right to lord it over everyone else. But now, while they retained Belgrade as well as suzerainty over

Wallachia and Moldavia, they surrendered much of Hungary, Croatia and Poland, recovering Podolia, including the demolished fortress at Kaminets, which, for twenty-seven years after the attack, had served as the regional base of their rule. Ottoman power waned, the disaster at Vienna and the humiliating treaty followed by janissaries ruthlessly creating havoc in the sultanate. After the Vienna defeat they had dethroned and jailed Mehmed IV: then they did the same to Mustafa II in 1703 and Ahmed III in 1730. They then had Selim III stabbed to death in 1807, and the next year strangled Mustafa IV at the behest of Mustafa's brother.

As well as being driven back in Hungary, Croatia and Poland, the Muslims could not control their vassal rulers in other provinces, though Greece did not gain independence until 1832, Lord Byron having died of marsh fever in 1824 in the town of Missolonghi after joining the Greek uprising. Exactly two years later most of the residents of Missolonghi, besieged by Ottoman forces, tried to make a break for it but were massacred.

The issue of the Ottoman occupation of Balkan lands led in the 1870s to a series of international crises. Beginning with an insurrection against Turkish rule in Herzegovina and Bosnia in July 1875, rebellion swept the Balkans. In 1876 there was a brutal Turkish suppression of a Bulgarian uprising as well as fighting and massacres elsewhere and a declaration of war on the Muslims by Serbia and Montenegro.

The Russian public reacted strongly to these developments. Pan-Slavism, up till then except for small circles of intellectuals no more than a vague sentiment, for the first time became an active force. Pan-Slav committees sent 5,000 volunteers, ranging from simple peasants to prominent members of society, including 800 former Russian army officers, to fight in the Serbian army, which was entrusted to one of the leading Russian military volunteers, a general.

But the Turks defeated the Serbs, hence the last hope of Balkan nationalities in their uneven contest with the Ottomans rested on Russian intervention. The Russian government considered intervention carefully and without enthusiasm. The international situation, with the United Kingdom and Austria-Hungary hostile to Russia, argued against war, as did the internal conditions, for military reforms were being enacted.

Besides, responsible tsarist officials did not believe at all in Pan-Slavism, the main exception being the Russian ambassador to Constantinople. But as the Balkan struggle continued, as international diplomacy failed to bring peace and as Russia became gradually more deeply involved in the conflict, the tsarist government, having come to an understanding with Austria-Hungary, on 24 April 1877 declared war on the Ottomans.

The war was difficult, bitter and costly, highlighted by such engagements as four battles as the Russians and Bulgarian volunteers known as *opalchentsi* fought the Muslims for control of the key Shipka pass in the Balkan mountains and the Turkish defence of the fortress of Plevna, which the Russians initially assaulted three times and were repelled with a loss of 30,000 men before starting systematic siege operations. With the capture of Turkish positions cutting off all communications from Plevna, the city was completely isolated. It would have been wiser for the commander to abandon it and preserve his army for use in the later stages of the war but he had explicit orders from the sultan to hold out. This became a hopeless task. On 9 December he made a desperate sortie in an attempt to break through the Russian lines but was defeated, and on the following day he surrendered.

The siege had delayed further Russian advances by five months but after this triumph and victory in the fourth battle for the Shipka pass the coalition eventually prevailed, pushing the Ottomans back all the way to the gates of Constantinople. Tsarist soldiers were approaching the Turkish capital when fighting ceased and they withdrew, to the relief of the British government, which had been party to a protocol whose rejection by the Turks had brought about the conflict. But though it could not object to Russia's declaration of war, it had watched with alarm the progress of the tsarist armies, and Queen Victoria and Prime Minister Disraeli bypassed the Foreign Office in order to warn the tsar against taking Constantinople. Victoria had pushed hysterically for war with Russia, her hatred of Russia preventing her from seeing that a constitutional monarch had to work with the government, not against it, and her attempt to pursue a foreign policy of her own eventually failed. The real enemy was not recognised. If it were not for her blind hatred of Russia, Constantinople could have been reclaimed from Islam instead of in 1930 being officially renamed Istanbul. For centuries the common vernacular Turkish word for Constantinople had been a garbled version of the Greek for 'into the city', *eis tin polin*.

A humiliating treaty reflected the utter Ottoman defeat. Turkey agreed to big territorial concessions. Bulgaria, as well as being enlarged, became fully autonomous; Serbia and Montenegro were recognised as fully independent, as was Romania, which had fought jointly with Russia at Plevna; Bosnia and Herzegovina were to receive a large degree of autonomy; and Turkey was to pay a huge indemnity.

The Ottomans had lost the military initiative. And, following their defeat as an ally of Germany in 1918 their empire ended with a 1923 treaty in Lausanne.

At last, Europe was free of the menace of Islam. Muslims could be dismissed as lacking ambition and far away. Over the rest of the world, too, an enfeebled Islam ceased to be a threat. So much suffering all over the world for a thousand years! So much aggression for so many centuries! So much humiliation and degradation! If only the Arabs had stayed in their desert! Scholars have estimated that in their thousand-year assault on the rest of humanity the Muslims killed 650 million non-Muslims. Such a number is comprehensible only to astrophysicists and palaeontologists. Jupiter is 485 million miles away and the beginning of the Cambrian period, the age before the dinosaurs, 541 million years ago. And most of those slain had relatives and other loved ones who grieved.

Those thousand years were an unacknowledged prolonged holocaust. Between 711 and 1700 Europe fought dozens of major wars to keep Islam at bay, and individual countries had to wage hundreds of bloody regional wars to protect themselves from Muslim aggression. A thousand years of hostility: that is the true story of Islam. One cannot understand Islam's history without knowing this. Muslims' imaginary virtues are praised and envied by ignorant civilised people. Everyone defends Islam; few have read the *Koran*. Western Europe has forgotten

Barbarossa; the 1565 Siege of Malta; the conquest of Cyprus 169

history. It is as though a strange amnesic fog has swept across its lands, smothering all folk memory, a mist causing an epidemic of forgetting. The past is rarely discussed. And ignorance of the past leads fatally to misunderstanding of the present.

On an epic journey lasting from 1325 to 1354 that began as a pilgrimage to Mecca, Ibn Battuta visited Persia, Mesopotamia, Asia Minor, Central Asia, southern Spain ('Al-Andalus'), India, China, Sumatra, north Africa, Arabia, Malaysia, Afghanistan, the Caucasus, Turkey (Anatolia), Somalia, Tanzania and Mali. Towns visited included Bukhara and Timbuktu. He travelled 75,000 miles and called this vast disparate area *'Dar al-Islam'*, the Abode of Islam. Everywhere he went he found himself among people with cosmopolitan attitudes and backgrounds similar to his own. He passed from one territory to the next as though strolling along a broad highway that stretched from Morocco to Mecca. It was lined with hostels, colleges, madrasas and mosques where he met a confraternity of scholars, judges (he was himself by profession a jurist), pilgrims and other travellers, everyone speaking in classical Arabic as a lingua franca. In a 1986 study, Ross Dunn wrote that Ibn Battuta 'regarded himself as a citizen not of a country called Morocco, but of the *Dar al-Islam*, to whose universalist spiritual, moral and social values he was loyal above any other allegiance'. Muslims have always imagined a binary opposition between the Muslim and non-Muslim world, a pair of categories that divides the world into two zones, one where the principles of Islamic law are in force, and one where they are not. The other zone is *Dar al-Harb* – the Abode of War. Hassan al-Banna, founder of the Muslim Brotherhood, one of the biggest and most influential Islamic revivalist organisations, said in 1924, 'Peace is when the whole world is Muslim.'

Dar al-Harb, the Abode of War, means anywhere Islam has not yet conquered. And, following a thousand years of *jihad*, Muslims, having read in the *Koran* (4:100) that 'He who leaves his home in the cause of Allah will find on the earth many locations and great abundance', have now adopted the other hallowed tactic in the plan for world domination – *hijra*, migration.

Quotes from the *Koran*

2:291 'Slay the unbelievers wherever you find them.'

3:28 'Let not believers make friends with infidels.'

3:85 'He that chooses a religion other than Islam, it will not be accepted from him and in the world to come he will surely be among the losers.'

4:101 'The unbelievers are your inveterate enemies.'

4:145 'Believers, do not choose the infidels rather than the faithful for your friends.'

5:33 'Those that criticise Islam shall be slain or crucified or have their hands and feet cut off on alternate sides.'

5:51 'Believers, take neither the Jews nor the Christians for your friends.'

5:80 'You see many making friends with unbelievers. Evil is that to which their souls prompt them. They had incurred the wrath of Allah and shall endure eternal torment.'

5:86 'Those who disbelieve and deny Our revelations shall become the inmates of Hell.'

8:12 'Allah revealed His will to the angels, saying, "I shall be with you. Give courage to the believers, I shall cast terror into the hearts of the infidel. Strike off their heads, strike off the very tips of their fingers!"

8:14 'The scourge of the Fire awaits the unbelievers.'

8:39 'Make war on them [unbelievers] until... Allah's religion shall reign supreme.'

8:60 'Muslims must gather all weapons to terrorise the infidels.'

8:65 'If there are twenty steadfast men among you, they shall vanquish two hundred; and if there are a hundred, they shall rout a thousand infidels, for they are stupid.'

9:5 'Fight and kill the disbelievers wherever you find them, take them captive, harass them, lie in wait and ambush them using every stratagem of war.'

9:28 The infidels are unclean. Do not let them approach a mosque.'

9:29 'Fight those who do not embrace the true Faith until they pay tribute out of hand [the *jizya* tax] and are utterly subdued.'

9:38-41 Believers, why is it that when you are told: 'March in the cause of Allah', you linger slothful in the land?...If you do not go to war, He will punish you sternly...Whether unarmed or well-equipped, march on and fight for the cause of Allah, with your wealth and with your persons.'

9:123 'Believers, make war on the infidels who dwell around you.'

13:34 'Punishment awaits them [unbelievers] in this nether life: but more grievous is the punishment of the life to come.'

13:35 The Fire shall be the end of the unbelievers.'

22:19 'Garments of fire have been prepared for the unbelievers. Scalding water shall be poured upon their heads, melting their skins and that which is in their bellies. They shall be lashed with rods of iron.'

47:4 'Do not yearn for peace with the infidels. Behead them when you catch them.'

Translations by N.J. Dawood in the Penguin Classics revised 1997 edition of *The Koran*.

Quotes on Islam

- **A thousand years ago, Zakariya Razi,** a Persian chemist, philosopher and physician, sometimes called Rhazes, wrote, 'If the people of this religion [Islam] are asked about the proof for the soundness of their religion, they flare up, get angry and spill the blood of whoever confronts them with this question. They forbid rational speculation, and strive to kill their adversaries. This is why truth became thoroughly silenced and concealed.'
- **In 1300, Marco Polo** wrote, 'All the Muslims in the world are agreed in wishing ill to all the Christians in the world.'
- **In the eighteenth century, John Wesley,** founder of Methodism, wrote, 'Ever since the religion of Islam appeared in the world, the espousers of it have been as wolves and tigers to all other nations, rending and tearing all that fell into their merciless paws, and grinding them with their iron teeth; that numberless cities are razed from the foundation, and only their name remaining; that many countries, which were once as the garden of God, are now a desolate wilderness; and that so many once numerous and powerful nations are vanished from the earth! Such was, and is at this day, the rage, the fury, the revenge, of these destroyers of humankind.'
- **In 1831, Samuel Coleridge** the poet warned that the foundation of a temporal kingdom under the guise of a spiritual authority was effected in full by the early Muslims 'to the establishment of the most extensive and complete despotism that ever warred against civilisation and humanity's interests'.
- **In 1861, Sir William Muir,** orientalist and historian, wrote, 'Islam is the most stubborn enemy of Civilisation, Liberty and Truth the world has yet known.'

- **In 1877, William Gladstone,** four times prime minister, said, 'The *Koran*, an accursed book. So long as there is this book there will be no peace in the world.'
- **In 1938, Hilaire Belloc,** Anglo-French writer and historian, wrote, 'It is dangerous that westerners have forgotten all about Islam. They have never come in contact with it. They take for granted that it is decaying, and that, anyway, it is just a foreign religion which will not concern them. Islam very nearly destroyed us. It is the most formidable and persistent enemy our civilisation has had, and may at any moment become as large a menace in the future as it has been in the past. There will probably be a resurrection of Islam and our grandchildren will see a renewal of that tremendous struggle between the Christian culture and what has been for more than a thousand years its greatest opponent.'

Bibliography

Aslanyan, Anna (2021), *Dancing on Ropes: Translators and the Balance of History*. London: Profile Books.
Braudel, Fernand (1949), *The Mediterranean and the Mediterranean World in the Age of Philip II*. New York: Harper & Row.
Balfour, Patrick & Kinross, Baron (1977), *The Ottoman Centuries: The Rise and Fall of the Turkish Empire*. London: Perennial.
Bancroft, Richard, Archbishop (chief overseer) (1611), *The Bible*, authorised version. London: Robert Barker.
Barbaro, Nicolò (trans. John Melville-Jones) (1969), *Diary of the Siege of Constantinople*. New York: Exposition. Posted on the website of De Re Militari, the Society for Medieval History, on 23 August 2016.
Benedictow, Ole J. (2021), *The Complete History of the Black Death*. Suffolk: Boydell & Brewer.
Bridge, Anthony (1988), *Suleiman the Magnificent; Scourge of Heaven*. New York: Hippocrene Books.
Chatterton, Edward Keble (1909), *Sailing Ships*. London: Sidgwick & Jackson.
Clark, Malcolm (2003), *Islam for Dummies*. New Jersey: John Wiley & Sons.
Collins, Roger (2012), *Caliphs and Kings: Spain, 796-1031*. New Jersey: John Wiley & Sons.
Dawood, N.J. (trans.) (1997), *The Koran*. London: Penguin Classics.
——, (trans.) (1973), *Tales from the Thousand and One Nights*. London: Penguin Classics.
Davis, Robert (2003), *Christian Slaves, Muslim Masters: White Slavery in the Mediterranean, the Barbary Coast and Italy, 1500-800*. London: Palgrave Macmillan.
Defoe, Daniel (1719), *Robinson Crusoe*. London: William Taylor.
Dunn, Ross (1986), *The Adventures of Ibn Battuta*. University of California Press.
Dupuy, R.E. & T.N. (1993), *The Collins Encyclopedia of Military History*. New York: BCA.
Fisher, Sir Godfrey (1957), *Barbary Legend: War, Trade and Piracy in North Africa 1415-1830*. Oxford: Clarendon Press.
Fremont-Barnes, Gregory (2006), *The Wars of the Barbary Pirates*. London: Osprey.

Gil, Moshe (1992), *A History of Palestine, 634-1099*. Cambridge University Press.
Hasan al-Rammah (1260s), *Book of Military Horsemanship and Ingenious War Devices*. Syria.
Haynes, Alan (1994), *The Gunpowder Plot*. Stroud: Sutton.
Juvaini (1240s), *History of the World Conqueror*.
Kazhdan et al (ed.) (1991), *Oxford Dictionary of Byzantium*.
Mann, Thomas (trans. John E. Woods) (2005), *Joseph and his Brothers*. New York: Alfred A. Knopf (Everyman's Library).
Menocal, Maria Rosa (2003), *The Ornament of the World*. London: Little, Brown.
Meynard, Charles Barbier de (trans.) (1865), *Des Routes et des Provinces*. Paris: *Journal Asiatique*.
Muir, Sir William (1896), *Mameluke Dynasty of Egypt*. London
Norwich, John Julius (1999), *A Short History of Byzantium*. New York: Vintage. (2017) *Four Princes*. London: John Murray.
Parker, Geoffrey (ed.) (1993), *The Times Atlas of World History*, fourth edition. London: BCA.
Penzer, N.M. (2005), *The Harem: Inside the Grand Seraglio of the Turkish Sultans*. New York: Dover Publications.
Pipes, Daniel (1981), *Slave Soldiers and Islam: The Genesis of a Military System*. New Haven: Yale University Press.
Polo, Marco (1298/9), *The Travels*. (Trans.) Robert Latham (1958), Harmondsworth: Penguin.
Seton-Watson, Hugh (1967), *The Russian Empire 1801-1917*. Oxford University Press.
Shakespeare, William (1598, 1603, 1622), *The Merchant of Venice, Othello, Macbeth*. London.
Simovic, Ljubomir (1989), *The Battle of Kosovo*. Belgrade.
Strachey, Lytton (1928), *Elizabeth and Essex*. London: Chatto & Windus.
Sturluson, Snorri (1260), *King Harald's Saga*. (Trans. Magnus Magnusson and Hermann Pálsson) (1966). Harmondsworth: Penguin Classics.
Temperley, Harold W.V. (1919), *History of Serbia*. Forgotten Books Classic Reprint, 2018.
Tracy, Larisa (ed.) (2013), *Castration and Culture in the Middle Ages*. Martlesham: D. S. Brewer.
Trevelyan, G.M. (1967), *English Social History*. Harmondsworth: Pelican Books.
Van de Weyer, Robert (2002), *The Shared Well*. Washington: Brassey's.
Waqidi, al- (eighth century), *Book of History and Campaigns*. Baghdad.
Waltari, Mika (1952), *The Dark Angel*. (Trans.) Naomi Walford (1953), London: Putnam.

Webb, Simon (2020), *The Forgotten Slave Trade: The White European Slaves of Islam*. Barnsley: Pen & Sword History.

Wilson, Jean & Roehrborn, Claus (1944), 'Long-Term Consequences of Castration in Men: Lessons from the Skoptzy and the Eunuchs of the Chinese and Ottoman Courts', *The Journal of Clinical Endocrinology & Metabolism*, Vol. 84, Issue 12, 1 December 1999, pp. 4324-31.

Ziegler, Philip (1997), *The Black Death*. London: The Folio Society.

Index

Abbas I, Muslim ruler of the Safavid Persians 155-6
Abd al-Rahman, in 756 founds a new Arab dynasty in Spain with enormous bloodshed 34
Abd ar-Rahman, 7th-century Arab merchant, 5, 7-8, 10, 12
Abul Abbas, 'the Blood-shedder', founds the Abbasid caliphate 33
Abu Jafar, Abul Abbas's brother and successor, equally cruel and treacherous, who adopts the title al-Mansur, 'the Victorious', and founds Baghdad 33
Acre 67
Adrianople 83-5, 89
Afghanistan 53, 169
Ager Sanguinis, Battle of 59
Ahmad ibn Arabsha (1389-1450), writer and traveller 81
Aikin, John (1747-1822), author 33-4
Ain Jalut, Battle of 65
Alamut castle, Assassins' headquarters 62
Algarve 32
Algeria 51
Al-Lat, a god 11
Allah, another god 7-8, 28-30, 32, 34, 48, 50-1, 64, 73, 86, 89-90, 95, 111-12, 114, 119, 125, 134, 151, 169-71
Almoravids and Almohads; successive Berber dynasties 45, 46
Al-Nasir, Almohad caliph 46
Alp Arslan, Seljuk sultan 55-6
Al-Tabari, historian 35, 38
Amorium, second city of Byzantine empire 38-40
Amr ibn al-As, Arab commander 25

Anatolia, roughly modern Turkey 23, 39, 51, 55, 58, 68-9, 72, 81-2, 112, 123-4, 143, 156, 169
Antioch 23-4, 59, 61, 67
Arabia 1, 6, 11-12, 17-18, 20, 23-4, 41, 169
Armada, Spanish 148, 150
Assassins 62-3
Astrakhan 143
Asturias, mountain range in north Spain 30
Atlantic, stopped Islam's western expansion 30
Aybeg, first Mamluke sultan 65
Ayla, important Christian tribe in south Syria 17

Baghdad 33, 38, 40-2, 53, 55, 61, 64, 81
Baltimore, Irish village raided for slaves by Barbary corsairs 151
Barbarossa, corsair admiral 135-6
Barbary Coast corsairs 149
Batu, Mongolian khan 63
Baybars, Mamluke sultan 66-7
Balkans 73-4, 77, 121, 129, 166
Baltoglu, Ottoman admiral 98, 101-2
Bashi-bazouks, Ottoman cannon fodder 78, 85, 112, 118, 124
Bavaria 160
Bayezid I, Ottoman sultan 75-83
Bayezid II, Ottoman sultan 124
Belgrade 76, 120, 127, 135, 140, 142, 164-5
Berbers 30-1, 45, 48
Beretta, gunmaker company 144
Berke, khan of the Golden Horde 64
Bible, the 27, 52
Billa, last Abbasid caliph 64-5

Black Death, the plague *Yersinia pestis* 72
Boabdil, last Moorish king of Granada 47
Boccaccio, Giovanni; Italian writer 72
Boleyn, Anne; wife of Henry VIII 3
Bosporus 35, 68, 83, 85, 101, 104
Bragadin, Marco; general slain in Cyprus 144
Buda 127, 132, 141, 155, 164
Bulgaria 67, 121, 133, 168
Byzantine empire 12, 16, 23, 34, 38, 58-9, 74, 85-6, 126

Caffa, Crimean port of Genoese merchants 69-72, 126
Cairo 41, 65-7
Canterbury Tales, The 72
Carthage 25
Cervantes, Miguel; Spanish novelist 145-6, 149
Chaldiran, Battle of 125
Chapuys, Eustace; Savoyard ambassador 3
Chaucer, Geoffrey; English poet 72
Charles, ruler of much of Gaul, called Martel, 'the Hammer', after halting Muslim expansion in West Europe 31
Chatterton, Edward Keble; naval military historian 136
China 33, 41, 66, 70, 82, 169
Christianity 32, 39, 48, 51, 76, 86, 116, 129, 145, 160
Christians 8, 12, 28, 37, 40, 42-3, 45-6, 48, 51-2, 67, 69-70, 80, 85-6, 99, 113, 116, 118-19, 129, 136, 138-9, 145, 148, 155
Chronicle of 754 30-1
Cid, El 45
Collins, Roger; historian of Spain 31
Comnenus, Manuel; Byzantine emperor 61
Constans II, Byzantine emperor 27
Constantine Copronymus, Byzantine emperor 34
Constantine XI, last Byzantine emperor 83-4, 87, 97, 104, 111, 116
Constantinople, fall of 86-119
Cornwall 150, 153
Crete 36-7, 129, 146
Cyprus 27, 143-6

Damascus 19, 22-3, 28, 45, 52, 65, 80
Danube 77, 85, 120, 122, 127, 130, 161, 163
Dardanelles (Hellespont) 85
Dark Angel, The 86
David IV, king of Georgia 60
Dazimon, Battle of 39
Defoe, Daniel; novelist 152
Decameron, The 72
Devereux, Robert, Earl of Essex 3
Dhimmitude, inferior status of Jews and Christians (*dhimmis*) 69
Didgori, Battle of 60
Dhu Khalasa, a god 17
Djerba, Battle of 137,
Dome of the Rock, shrine in Jerusalem 29
Don Quixote 145
Doria, Andrea; Genoese admiral 135-6
Dracula, gothic novel 122, named after...
...Draculea, called Vlad Țepeș – Vlad the Impaler 121-2
Drake, Francis 148
Ducas, Andronicus; Byzantine military governor 57, 58
Dumat al-Jandal, Christian tribe in north Arabia in 7th century 7

Egypt 24-5, 28-30, 32, 41, 43, 51-2, 64-5, 125-6, 143
Elizabeth and Essex 4
English Channel 80, 148, 150, 153
Ertugrul, Turkmen warlord, Othman's father 69
Euphemius, admiral of Sicily's fleet before running off with a nun 36

Fatimid dynasty 41
Ferdinand, Habsburg ruler of Royal Hungary 132, 135
Ferdinand II of Aragon 47
France 3, 34, 52, 71, 79, 126, 164

Galley slaves 148, 151
Garnet, Henry; Jesuit martyr 48
Gallipoli 73-4, 83, 86, 128
Germany 77, 168

Index   179

Ghassan, big Christian tribe along the Syrian/Arabian border in 7th century 19
Gibraltar 30, 48
Golden Horn 85, 88, 91, 98, 100, 104, 119
Greater Zab, Battle of 33
Greece 38, 68, 75, 124, 135, 166
Greek fire 28, 32, 61, 100-1, 108, 118

Habsburg empire 137
Hafiz ibn al-Hajar, 15th-century historian 20
Hardradi, Harald 58-59
Harems 43-4
Hawazin tribe 10-11
Henry IV 80
Henry VIII 3, 130, 147
Heraclius, Byzantine emperor 12, 17, 19, 23
Hindu Kush 54, 80
Homs, Syrian town 71
Homs, Battle of 67
Harun Rashid, Abbasid caliph 35
Hormuzan, Sassanid commander 26
Hulagu, Mongol leader 63-5
Hungary 84, 120-1, 126-7, 129, 132, 135, 137, 154-5, 160, 164, 166-7
Hunyadi, John; general, *then* regent of Hungary 120-1, 127

Ibn Abdulla, founder of emirate in Morocco 41
Ibn Battuta, traveller 42, 169
Ibn Kathir, influential scholar 11, 50
Ibn Masud, compiler of early version of the *Koran* 29
Il-Ghazi, best known for his drinking, his victory at the 1119 Battle of Ager Sanguinis and his following defeat at the Battle of Didgori 59-60
India 29, 31, 53-5, 80, 169
Ireland 151, 153
Iron Bridge, Battle of the 24
Isabella of Castile 47

Jadhima, tribe in 7th-century Arabia 8-9
Janissaries 74, 78, 83, 92, 97, 113-16, 129, 131, 137, 141-2, 155-8, 162, 166

Janissary, etymology of word 74
Jerusalem 2, 22-3, 29, 51-2, 63
Jews 1-4, 6, 8, 12, 17, 45, 69
Jizya tax, a protection racket 8, 11-12, 16-17, 24-5, 34-5, 37, 42, 45, 69, 85
John of Capistrano, Franciscan friar 120
Jolly Roger pirate flag 136
Joseph and his Brothers 43
Jurash, ancient Arabian caravan town 12

Kahlenberg mountain, heights overlooking Vienna 163
Karakorum, Mongolian capital 63
Karlovitz, 1699 treaty of 165
Ket-Buka, Mongol commander 65-6
Khalid ibn al-Walid, Arab warrior 7-9, 11, 16-17, 20-4
Khaybar, Arabian oasis 6
Khotyn, Battle of 159
Kilij Arslan II, Seljuk sultan 61
Knighton, Henry; medieval chronicler 72
Koran, the 29, 50-3, 70, 111, 119, 133, 136, 142, 168-9
Kosovo Field, Battle of 74-5
Kublai, Great Khan 65
Kutuz, second Mamluke sultan 65-6

Lampedusa, Mediterranean island 35
Las Navas de Tolosa, Battle of 46
La Valette, Jean de; defenders' leader at the Siege of Malta 129-30, 137, 139-40
Lazar, Serbian prince 75
Leo IV, Byzantine emperor 34
Lepanto, Battle of 144, 146, 148
Libya 51
Liutprand, king of Lombardy 32
Louis of Hungary 126
Longo, Giovanni; soldier hero 85, 87-8, 92, 95-8, 104-6, 109-10, 113-15
Lvov, Siege of 159

Macbeth 49
Macedonia 75-6
Mafia, etymology of word 37
Maingre, Jean le; French soldier 78-80

Malik al-Salih, penultimate Ayyubid sultan 65
Malta, Siege of 137-140
Mamai, Golden Horde warlord 72
Mamlukes 38, 40-1, 43, 46, 52, 65
Mamlukes, as rulers 65-6, 143
Mann, Thomas; German novelist 43
Marmara, Sea of 68, 85, 91-2
Marrakesh 45-6
Marsala, Sicilian harbour 28
Martin Luther, influential German religious reformer 133
Matthias Corvinus, Hungarian king 121
Marwan II, last Umayyad caliph 32
Mary, Queen of Scots 4
Mazara, Sicilian port 36
Mavrocordato, Alexander; Ottoman diplomat 164-5
Medina 26
Mediterranean Sea 25, 27, 36, 38, 62, 129, 136-7, 143, 146-7, 150, 153
Mehmed I, Ottoman sultan 83
Mehmed II, Ottoman sultan 83-6, 91, 94, 103, 111, 113, 116-17, 120-4, 127
Merchant of Venice, The 140
Michael the Brave, Romanian hero ruler 154
Michael IX, Byzantine emperor 68
Mircea, ruler of Wallachia 78
Mohács, Battle of 130-2
Mongolia 63
Mongols 63-7, 70, 81-2, 126
Möngke, Great Khan 63, 65
Montenegro 123, 166, 168
Moriscos 48, 51, 151
Morocco 30, 41-2, 45, 51, 151-2, 169
Moses 2
Muawiya, founder of Umayyad dynasty 28
Muir, Sir William; historian 7, 64
Murad I, Ottoman sultan 74-5
Murad II, Ottoman sultan 83
Musa, Arab general 30
Mustafa, Kara; grand vizier at 1683 Siege of Vienna 160, 161-4
Mustafa, Lala; Ottoman commander in Cyprus 143

Mutawakkil, Muntasir, Mutaz and Muhtadi, Abbasid caliphs serially assassinated 40-1

Nahavand, Battle of 24, 26
Najran, Christian town in 7th-century Arabia 11
Nazareth 67
Nicopolis, Battle of 77-80
North Africa 25, 30, 32, 36, 38, 41, 45, 48, 67, 137, 151, 169
Nurbanu, powerful favourite wife of Selim II 142-3, 158

Obilić, Miloš; heroic assassin of Murad I 75
Orban, Hungarian iron founder, hoisted by his own petard at Vienna 84, 86, 93-4, 96, 112
Othman, founder of Ottoman empire 68-9, 73
Otranto, town on heel of Italy 123

Palmyra, Syrian town 22
Pera, port of Genoese merchants on Golden Horn 85, 95, 103-4, 119
Poland 77, 158-61, 166
Pole, Margaret; Catholic martyr 3
Praetorian Guard 40
Preveza, Battle of 135

Radu the Handsome, brother of Draculea 122-3
Rashid ad-Din Sinan, Assassin chief 62
Rawlinson, George; historian and theologian 26
Rhodes 27, 89, 127
Rhodes, Siege of 128-9
Rimpler, Georg; famous military engineer 162
Rizzo, Antonio; galley captain 84
Robinson Crusoe 152
Romania 78, 121, 168
Rome 40, 52, 77, 164
Russia and Russians 38, 43, 58, 143, 161, 165-8

St Augustine of Hippo 32
Safavid dynasty 124-5, 155-6
Salé, a bizarre republic 151-2
Saladin, sultan 52, 62-3
Sardinia 32
Sassanid empire 24, 26 30
Scylitzes, John; Greek historian 58
Selim I, Ottoman sultan 124-6
Selim II, Ottoman sultan 141-3
Selim III, Ottoman sultan 166
Seljuks 55-6, 59-61
Shajar ad Durr, first female Egyptian ruler since Cleopatra 65
Shakespeare, William 49, 112, 140, 144
Shipka, mountain pass in Bulgaria 167
Sigismund, king of Hungary 76-8
Slavery 6, 34-5, 42-3, 54, 67, 128, 150
Sobieski, Jan; heroic king of Poland 159, 160-5
Sokollu, Mehmed; Ottoman grand vizier 141-3, 145
Spain 30, 31-4, 41, 45-8, 51-2, 77, 144, 151, 169
Stoker, Bram; novelist 121
Strachey, Lytton; author 4
Suleiman 'the Magnificent', Ottoman sultan 125-42
Syria 7, 12, 15-17, 19, 21-4, 27-8, 32, 51, 62, 65, 67, 80, 82
Szeged, Siege of 140

Tabriz, Safavid capital 125, 156
Tadini, Gabriele; great military engineer 129
Takiya, Muslims' hallowed licence to lie 48, 50-1
Talas, Battle of 52
Tamar, queen of Georgia 61
Tarchaniotes, Byzantine general 56
Tariq, Muslim Berber commander 30
Tell Danith, Battle of 59
Theophilus, Byzantine emperor 38-40
Thousand and One Nights, The 35
Tigris river 38, 39
Tomori, Archbishop; Hungarian hero 130-1

Torah, the 2-3
Trevelyan, G. M.; historian 147
Tunisia 35, 51, 137
Turkey 23, 55, 168-9
Tusi, Nasir al-Din; 13th-century intellectual 64

Valletta, new Maltese capital, named after La Valette 140
Varangian Guard 58-9
Venice 44, 71, 86, 121, 136, 143-4, 148, 165
Vespucci, Amerigo; Italian merchant and explorer 47
Vienna 127, 133-5
Vienna, 1683 Siege of 160-6
Vikings 38, 43
Villiers de l'Isle Adam, Philippe; Grand Master of Knights of St John 127-9
Vladimir, prince of Kiev 43
Volga 143
Voltaire, French writer 140

Waqidi, al-; 8th-century historian 1, 7, 10, 13-14
Walford, Naomi; translator 86
Waltari, Mika; Finnish novelist 86
Wallachia, historical and geographical region of Romania 78, 122, 143, 154, 166
Wars of Apostasy 18-20
William of Rubruck, Flemish priest 63

Yamama, fortified town of rebel tribe in east-central Arabia in 7th century 20-1
Yarmuk river, Battle of 23
Yemen 11-12, 41
Yersinia pestis, plague 25, 71-2

Zápolya, John; Hungarian aristocrat put on the throne by the Ottomans 130, 132, 135
Zriny, Count Nicolas; while already badly wounded, head rammed in mouth of cannon by Ottoman captors and blown to smithereens 140-1
Zulfikar, legendary Ottoman scimitar 136